$5.-

MRS. EDWIN BERLINER

DEERFIELD LANE, ROCK RIDGE

MAMARONECK, NEW YORK

LIBRARY OF GREAT MUSEUMS

ART TREASURES OF THE PRADO MUSEUM

ART TREASURES OF THE

PRADO

MUSEUM

text by

HARRY B. WEHLE

Formerly Curator of Paintings, The Metropolitan Museum of Art

with a foreword by

F. J. SÁNCHEZ CANTÓN

Sub-Director, The Prado Museum

HARRY N. ABRAMS, INC., PUBLISHERS, NEW YORK

FIRST EDITION

Editor, MILTON S. FOX

Supervisor of Color Plates, WALTER NEURATH of Thames & Hudson, Ltd., London, England

---

TABLE OF CONTENTS

PHOTO DMITRI KESSEL (LIFE). COPYRIGHT TIME, INC.

LIST OF PLATES

(Arranged alphabetically by artist. All references are to plate numbers. Color plates are indicated by italic type.)

FOREWORD

IN THE FOREWORD to W. H. Boulton's *The Romance of the British Museum,* Sir Frederick Kenyon wrote: "The universe of man, like the universe of nature, extends its boundaries daily before our eyes; and it is in our museums that the story is displayed for the visitor to see."

The Prado unfolds the panorama of Spain's history while at the same time it presents masterpieces of a standard which is uniformly higher than any comparable collection can boast. There are on its walls no paintings to which the visitor can remain indifferent; he will encounter in its galleries few works of art that fail to move, delight, or instruct him.

This high level of quality is due to the fact that the Prado Museum, at the time of its creation in 1819 and in the ensuing years, had as its nucleus the paintings from the collections formed in the course of three centuries by the Kings of Spain. One may observe that in the royal succession, a taste for painting appears to have been a hereditary characteristic.

This love of painting and taste for art goes back as far as the thirteenth century. Sancho IV of Castile commissioned painters and paid them regular fees. His father Alfonso X the Wise, who died in 1284, had one of his miniaturists paint a panel showing a view of a shop where paintings were sold, as an illustration for the ninth of his *Canticles of the Virgin;* and in compiling his famous codex of laws, the *Siete Partidas,* he included a law regarding the ownership of a picture in a case where the panel on which it had been painted did not belong to the

painter. No parallel examples can be found in other countries.

The fondness of the Castilian court for painting continued during the fourteenth and fifteenth centuries. John II and Henry IV acquired Flemish panels, and Queen Isabella the Catholic collected pictures with such ardor and good taste that in a future edition of his famous and delightful book, *The Taste of Angels,* Mr. Francis Henry Taylor will have to devote a special chapter to her.

It is easy to demonstrate the persistence of this love of painting on the part of the Spanish Kings. The Emperor Charles V was a patron of Titian's; Philip II, as a well-informed amateur rather than simply a Mycenas, bought tirelessly in Italy and Flanders; Philip III enlarged the collections still further and brought Rubens to his court for an eight-month sojourn. Philip IV recalled this great painter of Antwerp to his service for half a year and sent Velázquez—his friend as well as his painter—to Italy twice, to buy masterpieces; and at the auction held after the death of Charles I of England, he acquired works of Mantegna, Raphael, and others. Charles II summoned all the forces that his congenital weakness could command to defend the artistic patrimony of the Crown. Philip V, to counteract the decline of Spain, engaged artists in France and bought hundreds of Dutch and Flemish genre and landscape paintings. Ferdinand VI and Charles III summoned to their court the Italians Amigoni, Giaquinto, and Tiepolo, and the Bohemian painter A. R. Mengs. Charles IV, while a prince, formed an admirable personal collection and gave employment to Goya. Ferdinand VII, with a stroke of generosity that serves to brighten his sorry memory, founded the Prado Museum, which his daughter Isabella II enlarged with further additions from the royal palaces and the Escorial.

On the other hand, despite the exemplary continuity of this tradition of collecting, the royal treasures were depleted through fires or wars. The Pardo Palace burned on March 13, 1604, and the Alcázar at Madrid on December 24, 1734, resulting in incalculable losses. Further lamentable destruction took place when the troops of the Archduke Charles of Austria were stationed in Madrid in 1710, during the War of the Spanish Succession, and a century later, during the Napoleonic occupation from 1808 to 1813; moreover the English, who at that time were Spain's allies, plundered the royal collections. The paintings which the Duke of Wellington recovered after the battle of Vitoria, as part of the effects of the claimant to the throne, were never restored to the Spanish Crown.

In addition to the royal collections that formed its nucleus, the Prado was further enriched by supplementary accessions from the convents suppressed during the nineteenth century, by gifts and bequests, and by purchases made by the State or by the Trustees of the Museum. These additions, however, have not substantially altered or modified the original character of the splendid collection formed by the Hapsburgs and the Bourbons. With scrupulous respect, they always obtained paintings from the European lands under their sovereignty—Flanders, Milan, Naples, and Sicily—either by inheritance, purchase, or exchange. Thanks to this policy, there is not a single picture in the Prado which entered Spain either haphazardly or by "right of conquest."

The Spanish school of painting was greatly influenced by the fact that the aesthetic tastes of the Kings, during the sixteenth and seventeenth centuries, were oriented towards the art of Venice and Flanders—the schools which provided our painters with their most fruitful models. Thus the visitor to the Prado can not only observe the development of the native styles but can also understand to a great extent how these were formed. Through studying the works of Giorgione, Titian, Veronese, Tintoretto, the Bassani, Rubens, Van Dyck, Bruegel, and Teniers, the Spanish painters acquired their own technical skill. The diverse influences of painters whom they admired, rather than slavishly copied, made the artists versatile in various realistic and idealized styles; thus Spain was delivered from direct and sterile imitation, and remained free from cold eclecticism or mannerism. The result of all this is that the Prado is endowed with a "functional vitality" which differentiates this museum from other collections of art.

The delight that Philip II took in the strange mode of painting practiced by the Flemish artists Bosch and Patinir; the long residence of El Greco in Spain—where he became a truly original artist; and the copiousness of Goya's works in this Museum, account for the fact that the Prado has been, is today, and will continue to be a fountainhead for great innovators in art, past, present, and future. How much Impressionism, Expressionism, and Surrealism all owe to the Prado!

But the Prado is much more than this: its name alone is sufficient to evoke Velázquez, that painter *par excellence*, the master without flaw.

The reader may familiarize himself with this extraordinary collection of pictorial beauty, and with the emotions and historical connotations it arouses, as he holds in his hands this beautiful book, with its learned and spirited text by my friend and colleague, Mr. Harry B. Wehle. It is an honor to sign the opening pages of this handsome publication with the title which I have held at the Museum since June, 1922.

F. J. Sánchez Cantón
Sub-Director of the Prado Museum

14

THE PRADO MUSEUM

Its Paintings, and a Brief History

THE PRADO MUSEUM in Madrid is so named because of the wide parklike area or *Prado,* refreshed with trees and grass, beside which the Museum is situated. The building, a large and dignified pile, three stories in height and with enough columns to give it a modified classical style, was undertaken on order of the culture-loving king, Charles III, in 1785. He chose as his architect the distinguished Juan de Villanueva, and the structure was planned to house a museum of natural history. But Charles died in 1788 and the years passed—years of indolence, of famine, of invasion. Thus the building remained incomplete and even became somewhat dilapidated. In 1814, after the Peninsular War, Ferdinand VII returned from France to reoccupy the Spanish throne, and soon married his second wife, Doña María Isabel de Braganza. According to the accounts one reads, he had moved most of the paintings out of the great Royal Palace simply to relieve the confusion and to facilitate the refurbishing of the interior before his bride arrived. The idea of using Charles III's Natural History Museum, founding there a museum of art, seemed normal enough, for the precedent existed of the Musée du Louvre in Paris, which had been opened only twenty-five years before. At first Ferdinand thought of having the new museum named for himself, the Museo Ferdinandino. According to Enriqueta Harris (*The Prado,* London and New York, The Studio, 1940), its purpose, besides the primary one of preserving surplus paintings and sculptures from the Royal Palace and from the palace at Aranjuez, was "for the teaching and profit of pupils and professors as well as to satisfy the noble curiosity of natives and foreigners and give to Spain the glory that she so justly deserves." Except in rainy weather the collection was to be on view Wednesdays from 9 to 2. Thirty-one great paintings containing nudes were kept at the Academy of San Fernando and were only for the eyes of professional artists. The prudish Charles III and Charles IV, and now Ferdinand VII, had moments of wishing them burned.

Ferdinand's young Queen, who was his niece as well as his second wife, fell in with the museum project enthusiastically, dedicating to it a great deal of her time and also a good deal of her personal capital. In the Prado today there is a portrait of her by Bernardo López, in which she is shown standing beside a window and gesturing toward the Museum building beyond. Beside her on the table lie plans for hanging the separate galleries. On November 19, 1819, however, when the august inauguration ceremony finally took place, poor María Isabel was not present, for she had died in childbirth almost a year before, and a new Queen some eight years her junior was officiating in her stead.

In the beginning there were exhibited at the Prado only 311 pictures, entirely drawn from the various royal palaces. All of them were by Spanish painters. Goya, already a man of seventy-three, was represented by two paintings, the remarkable full-length portrait of fumbling Charles IV and that of his hard-eyed Queen, María Luisa. Since its inauguration the Prado has undergone more than one remodeling to adapt it better to its function, and the collection of

15

paintings, which already numbered nearly two thousand by 1850, has now been increased by several hundred. Perhaps eighty percent of the collection is usually kept on exhibition.

Repeated visits to the Prado to see these pictures are apt to give the visitor a sense of having acquired, by a sort of osmosis, at least the commencement of an understanding of Spain's ardent yet humane and dignified spirit. The incomparable collection of paintings by Velázquez and Goya alone must be profoundly moving and instructive for even the comparatively fast-moving tourist. More than a century ago the indomitable traveler, George Borrow, in *The Bible in Spain*, wrote, "I will say for the Spaniards that in their social intercourse no people in the world exhibit a juster feeling of what is due to the dignity of human nature, or better understand the behavior which it behooves a man to adopt toward his fellow beings. It is one of the few countries in Europe where poverty is not treated with contempt, and, I may add, where the wealthy are not blindly idolized."

GOYA AND VELÁZQUEZ, yes, but Ribera and Zurbarán too, have as their common denominator a probity and an intelligence that lead them to examine their subjects with a scalpel's unflinching penetration, yet with an understanding and impartiality that breed charity. Theirs is a democracy that can see good even in kings, when there is good to be seen. Someone has remarked that Goya's verdict of Charles IV and his Queen foretells accurately the final estimate of history and likewise the eternal judgment when the last trumpet shall sound.

To offer a merely numerical account of the several greatest artists and their works in the Prado obviously would not give an estimate of the importance of what visitors find when they get there. Almost all of Velázquez' greatest paintings, about fifty altogether, are present: *The Surrender of Breda, The Topers,* the several royal equestrian portraits, the fascinating likenesses of the court dwarfs and buffoons, the portrait of Queen Mariana, *The Maids of Honor* (*Las Meninas*), and *The Spinners* (*Las Hilanderas*).

The Goyas, numbering 114 paintings and 480 drawings, may sound overabundant. But experience proves the contrary, for Goya had such a number of ideas and methods that the beholder never

seems to get enough of him and his works. The 50 Riberas, not all equally interesting, are at their best profoundly impressive and highly original. Yet with this master, as with El Greco, one must still take a journey if one is really to know his paintings, for the greatest Riberas are in the monastery of San Martino, overlooking Naples.

At the Prado, after all, the Spanish painters are only half the story. The 36 Titians, some in the lyric early vein and more from his richly orchestrated late period, are probably unequaled elsewhere. Rubens likewise, during his great, late years, devoted himself almost entirely to supplying the insatiable demands of the Spanish kings. Serious students of these painters find it absolutely obligatory to visit the Prado.

As in the cases of Velázquez and Goya, Titian and Rubens, there are other masters best seen at the Prado, although represented by fewer works. Hieronymus Bosch with seven paintings is better studied in the Prado than anywhere else, and the same statement can safely be made about Patinir with only four. The fifteen portraits by Anthonis Mor constitute the finest group of his works anywhere.

The 32 El Grecos in the Prado are highly exciting, although some of them are unable to make themselves clearly heard because their voices still remain hushed, as it were, under discolored varnish. With characteristic Spanish candor and insight, the distinguished Sub-Director, Don F. J. Sánchez Cantón, judges that "all in all, El Greco's religious works in the Prado must give way in importance to those in Toledo and the Escorial, whereas the series of portraits can have no possible equal." Much the same could be said of Zurbarán, whose vitality and beauty are seen in great paintings in the Prado, but who cannot be truly appreciated without a visit to the monastery at Guadalupe and to the museums at Seville and Grenoble. For Murillo, too, one must go to Seville, although the Prado has a numerous and wonderful showing of this currently undervalued artist.

It is probably not too rash, then, to suppose that most serious visitors to the Prado discover for themselves the principle that where an artist is of the first magnitude, his works may be enjoyed in any quantity whatsoever. The latest two or three generations of museum directors and collectors generally have shown a passionate interest in judiciously balanced art-historical collections. The Spanish monarchs, on the contrary, paid little attention to such

16

methodical procedures, giving expression instead to an engrossing appetite for art itself and amassing as many paintings as possible by the artists whose works afforded them the deepest satisfaction. These much intermarried members of the Austrian Hapsburg family and, after the year 1700, of the Bourbon line, these apparently unlovely and uninspired individuals—as revealed by their portraits and by the historical accounts of their unremitting wars and their incontinent efforts to control by force the minds of their subjects—these royal individuals, surprisingly enough, scored an unbeaten record as collectors of what is most glorious and enduring in art. These kings and queens ruling Spain from the end of the fifteenth century into the nineteenth showed a marked inclination to buy paintings by their own contemporaries, but their tastes were not fenced in by national boundaries. Thus, in periods when they found Spanish art not to their taste, they bought elsewhere, with the result that the officials at the Prado today are having uphill work of offsetting the shortage of fine fifteenth- and sixteenth-century Spanish paintings, which have only become generally appreciated in our own time.

A S WE HAVE SEEN, then, the Prado Museum was a royal undertaking, and for the first half century of its official existence the royal family paid the cost of its maintenance. It was not until 1868, after the dethronement of Isabella II, that the title *Real Museo* (Royal Museum) was changed to *Museo del Prado de Madrid*. Although this changing of its name announced a very real diminution of responsibility for the Museum on the part of subsequent Spanish rulers, it did not signify that further treasures were necessarily to be withheld. Further treasures did in fact arrive, including the many refreshing tapestry cartoons by Goya, which had lain neglected in the storeroom at the Royal Palace. Indeed, as recently as the 1940s the government of Generalissimo Franco has transferred to the Prado, permanently one hopes, several extremely fine paintings which since the time of Philip II had been in the vast monastery of San Lorenzo del Escorial. There they were comparatively inaccessible, and in any case surrounded by an incompatible weight of masonry. In the words of Havelock Ellis, "A disconcerting little stream of cosmopolitan tourists is forever passing through the temple . . . but it cannot wash away the deathly solemnity of this ferocious Escorial."

Yet the facts about the formation and enrichment of the Prado Museum serve to underline the fundamental circumstance that its collection, in its numerical aspect and likewise in its overwhelming quality, is the contribution of the royal rulers of Spain. The art of the Iberian Peninsula in ancient times and during the first fourteen centuries of the Christian era makes an unusually fascinating study, for there the succession of impinging civilizations and artistic influences was more complex and various than in most lands. It was not from the arts of those centuries, however, that the Spanish monarchs built their collections. If they were more interested in the present than in the past, they were also better aware of art that flourished beyond the Pyrenees than the difficulties of early travel would lead one to suppose. Even as late as the 1902 edition of Murray's *Handbook* (based on that of Richard Ford), we find a vivid picture of the hardships that travelers might expect to encounter in most parts of Spain which were off the beaten track.

Nevertheless, early in the fifteenth century, the courts of Spain seem to have been well aware of the art of the Van Eyck brothers. It was in 1428–29, after Hubert van Eyck had died, that his more famous brother Jan was sent to Portugal by Philip the Good, Duke of Burgundy, as a member of a delegation whose task it was to investigate the suitability of Princess Isabella as a prospective wife for the Good Duke. After the delegation's report, including her portrait by Van Eyck, had been sent home, there followed a delay of many months before the Duke's favorable response set the delegation free to return to the North, taking Isabella with it. Evidently Van Eyck had taken advantage of those months of waiting to visit some of the Spanish courts, and the Prado's elaborate Christian allegory, *The Fountain of Living Water* (plate 74), considered by many to be an early copy of a lost painting by the Van Eycks, is usually associated with this mission.

In Naples and Sicily at about that time, the Aragonese rule probably brought with it nearly as much of artistic value as it took away. Alfonso X at any rate took nothing back to Spain, for the culture of Naples appealed to him so strongly that he declined to return to Saragossa. In Castile, meanwhile, under Juan II the court encouraged letters and the other arts.

In 1479, when at last most of centrifugal Spain became united under Ferdinand of Aragón and Isabella of Castile, a determined effort was made to dislodge the Moors from Granada, their last foothold in Spain; and when this attack succeeded, in 1492—the year in which Columbus discovered America—the victory was celebrated throughout Christendom. In London a special *Te Deum* was sung in Saint Paul's. Moved probably by the mental weakness of their daughter, Joanna, called *Juana la loca* (because it was claimed that she was insane), the "Catholic Kings" founded what is said to be the earliest recorded mental hospital. They also expelled the Jews and established and ardently supported the Inquisition. They were thoroughly Spanish.

It was through Joanna's husband, Philip the Handsome of Austria, the son of Emperor Maximilian I, that the Hapsburgs made their appearance on the Spanish scene. The tradition of royal art patronage and informed art collecting was inculcated, more or less directly, by the connoisseurship of Maximilian, whose private prayerbook embellished with drawings by Cranach and Dürer, to mention but a single item, is one of the world's entrancing treasures. Isabella herself, besides promoting important architectural projects, built up a considerable collection of paintings, a good many of them inherited from her father. Of her pictures some at least were of the highest quality—works by Dieric Bouts, Rogier van der Weyden, Memling, and Botticelli. But in 1504, upon the death of Isabella, these treasures did not remain in the family, eventually to reach the Prado. Instead they went, appropriately enough, into the handsome Royal Chapel of the Cathedral of Granada, where they accompany the two imposing yet pathetic family sarcophagi, one with recumbent marble effigies of Ferdinand and Isabella, the other with those of Philip of Austria and Joanna "the Mad."

While Maximilian gave an impulse toward intelligent art collecting which was effectual for some three centuries, both in Spain and in Austria, he likewise demonstrated for the Hapsburgs the way toward "conquest by marriage." By means of this not entirely new sort of strategy, he for one had added to the Empire both Burgundy and the Netherlands, in the person of Mary of Burgundy, daughter of Charles the Bold, a lineage which incidentally was already famous for its patronage of art. Maximilian's brilliantly successful contempo-

raries, Ferdinand and Isabella, offered him through their offspring another valuable opportunity besides Doña Joanna, namely her brother Don Juan. In 1497 he was married to Maximilian's daughter, Margaret of Austria. The wedding took place in Salamanca, the guests being entertained with the performance of an up-to-date humanistic play about the God of Love. But, to quote the rich prose of the Hispanist, Georgiana Goddard King, "For Don Juan, the god he was to meet was not Eros, but his darker double Thanatos: the autumnal fevers seized him and in less than a fortnight he was dead."

Poor widowed Margaret of Austria, who soon suffered further tragic blows, must have felt a sense of relief when in 1507 she was given the responsibility of ruling the Netherlands. Until the time of her death in 1530 she continued as Regent, proving herself an excellent administrator. But historically her regency was perhaps less important than her role as aunt and educator of the young Charles, the son of Philip and Joanna, who had been born in 1500. His father died when Charles was six years old, and his mother had been banished to a convent.

AMONG THE MANY VALUABLE LESSONS which young Charles learned from his Aunt Margaret was the importance of art in the life of a great monarch. Two good, if minor, Northern painters, Master Michiel Sittow and Juan de Flandes, both of whom had previously worked at the court of Isabella the Catholic, now worked in Malines at the court of the Regent. Later she employed Jan Mostaert and Jan Vermeyen, both from the North Netherlands, and Bernaert van Orley who was appointed her Court Painter. She owned a book on human proportions by Jacopo de'Barbari which Dürer tried in vain to get from her when he went to view her collection on June 8, 1521, during his Netherlands sojourn. In his diary he reported having seen in her palace good paintings by Orley and Gossaert (Mabuse), and forty small oil paintings of "precision and excellence" by Juan de Flandes, twenty of which are now in the Palace in Madrid.

Apparently Dürer intended to give "Lady Margaret" a portrait which he had made of her father, the Emperor Maximilian, but Margaret expressed a strong dislike of it. Probably it was the portrait of 1519, now in the Kunsthistorisches Museum at Vienna. Besides quantities of tapestries and other decorative works, Margaret possessed paintings by Rogier van der Weyden, Memling, Bosch, and also the famous Van Eyck portrait of Arnolfini and his wife, now in the National Gallery, London. The Van Eyck was brought to Madrid in 1556 and remained there for two and a half centuries, until carried off as loot by the French during the Napoleonic invasion.

When Margaret died in 1530, she left most of her properties to Charles V, who although elected Emperor in 1510 had only now had himself crowned by the Pope at Bologna. When Ferdinand, his grandfather, died fourteen years earlier, Charles had become Charles I, King of Spain. This also included Spain's American colonies, Burgundy, the Netherlands, Austria, and the extensive parts of Italy under Hapsburg rule. Charles was an excessively busy ruler, the "head-foremost" monarch in Europe. By force of arms he proposed to protect his inheritance from competing monarchs, especially Francis I of France, but also there were necessary expeditions against the Moorish infidels in North Africa and the Turks in Hungary. Endlessly, too, there were troubles with the heretical Protestant princes of Germany, and the more powerful nobles in the Netherlands. Salvador de Madariaga, the Spanish historian and philosopher, calls attention to Charles's tolerance of at least partial political autonomy for the parts of his Empire, contrasting strangely with his unresting struggle to achieve absolute conformity in religious matters. His dearest wish, according to his own statement, was "for the peace and calm of Christendom, and the full use of the power which God had granted him against the heathen and the infidels." He was a leading figure at the Council of Trent, 1545–63, which launched the Counter Reformation.

Thus the Emperor would appear to have had little time for art. During the earlier part of his reign he patronized the artists to whom Margaret of Austria had accustomed him. It was in 1532, when in North Italy, that he first met Titian and thereupon realized that previously he had not been employing the greatest painters. He immediately made Titian a Knight of the Empire and in 1533 appointed him Court Painter. Two years later, when he decided on a punitive expedition against Tunis, he asked Titian to accompany him for the purpose of recording the events. But Titian declined the invitation, and the Emperor had to fall back on Vermeyen. Vermeyen's eight elaborate military epi-

sodes (later woven as tapestries) and probably also some views of battles in Germany, and some court portraits painted by him in Malines and Brussels, were hung in the Pardo Palace, a glorified hunting lodge at the edge of Madrid. There Philip II, the son of Charles V, and his successor, installed among other rooms a gallery of 47 royal portraits, all of three-quarter length and uniform in size. Among the portraits were 11 by Titian and 15 by Anthonis Mor, whose dignified and superbly constructed likenesses Charles continued to admire even after his discovery of Titian. Few, if any, of the portraits in this gallery survived the disastrous fire of 1604.

It appears clear that despite his obsession with performing what he considered his duties and with securing what he claimed to be his rights as the world's most powerful ruler, Charles managed also to give some attention to art. The Prado now possesses from his collection eight Titians, five Mors, one Cranach, and a beautiful triptych by Memling (plates 80, 81 & 94). Perhaps it was at his behest that his sister Maria of Hungary brought five additional Titians, and also Rogier van der Weyden's great *Descent from the Cross* (plate 91), when she came to Spain in 1556 after her years as successor to Margaret of Austria in the Netherlands. But there were undoubtedly more paintings still, for Charles is said to have owned six hundred. In determining the sources of most of the Prado's treasures, however, there are few documents to help beyond the infrequent inventories of the royal palaces.

Charles's urge to leave his imprint on the visual aspect of Spain is more clearly seen in his architectural enterprises than in his collection of paintings. In Madrid he rebuilt the immense, rambling Alcázar, which remained the chief royal residence until destroyed by fire in 1734. As a young man he had, although with misgivings, permitted the building of an ugly, up-to-date Spanish church within the grand old Moorish mosque at Cordova. A few years later, when he saw the result, he said sadly to the Cathedral chapter, "You have built what you or others might have built anywhere, but you have destroyed something that was unique in the world." In the same year, however, he himself decided to build a stone palace within the Alhambra enclosure at Granada, sacrificing part of the Moorish structure. The building, in a degraded Renaissance style, was never completed, but remains to this day a distressing incongruity.

When in 1556, worn out with a life of unremitting

activity and plagued by a hopeless illness, Charles relinquished his empire and retired to the convent at Yuste, in the western province of Estremadura, he took with him four Titians, including the gorgeous equestrian portrait of himself at the Battle of Mühlberg (plate 140), and *The Gloria,* a strange mystical view of the royal family kneeling before the heavenly throne. He took also Mor's portrait of the warped and unprepossessing Mary Tudor of England (plate 104), to whom he had recently given his son Philip in marriage. It is pleasant to remember that this grim and emaciated image hanging on his wall was at least partially offset by remarkably plentiful and delicious meals on his table, and Charles, despite his incurable illness, is reported to have been passionately fond of such mundane pleasures—and in surprisingly large portions.

W HEN HE RELINQUISHED THE CONTROL of his great empire, Charles wisely divided it into two parts, handing over Germany to his brother Ferdinand. Upon his son Philip II, not yet thirty years of age, he bestowed Spain, where he had personally spent comparatively little time and with whose language, according to some accounts, he was incompletely conversant. Together with Spain, Philip naturally received the vast Spanish American colonies. Less naturally he received Milan and Naples, and also the Netherlands, where the struggle against Protestantism had already gone far toward depleting the wealth of Spain, despite (or partly because of?) the gold and silver bullion which the ships from America continued to disgorge at Seville.

Perhaps it was because of the imperious character of his illustrious father that Philip had developed an inflexibly pious and reserved temperament and a neurotic inability to delegate power. As an act of religious devotion he built the immense, soul-chilling monastery and royal palace at El Escorial, finished in 1584 after twenty-six years of construction during which Philip was usually to be found on the premises, filled with new ideas and persistent "suggestions." In that generation Spain had produced no acceptable decorative painters except perhaps Navarrete, "the Dumb," and Philip was obliged to import such run-of-the-mill Italian artists as Luca Cambiaso, Federigo Zuccaro, and Pellegrino Tibaldi. The most impressive part of the

Escorial to many is the underground *Pantéon de los Reyes* or royal burial chamber, planned by Philip II for the black marble sarcophagi of the kings and queens of Spain; but it was not completed until seventy years later during the reign of his grandson Philip IV. Taken together with its descending staircase of dark, polished granite and its black, gleaming marble sarcophagi, it may be rated as probably the most triumphantly lugubrious room in existence.

Thus we see that in a very real sense Philip II occupied himself with aesthetic matters. Even while his father was alive, he had begun on his own responsibility to collect important paintings. From Titian he acquired at least 22, five now in the Escorial and 17 in the Prado. Two in the Prado— *Venus and Adonis* (with Adonis' face resembling Philip's own) and *Danaë and the Shower of Gold* (plate 141)—he ordered when he was only twenty-six years old. Both contain sumptuous female nude figures—surprisingly nude and sumptuous when we consider the extreme piety of Philip, and not to be explained simply by his youth, for fifteen to twenty years later he was still ordering from the ancient Venetian master such lush paintings as *The Fall of Man* (plate 153) and *Religion Succored by Spain* (plate 152). He also bought at least five famous *poesias* (Titian's own word for them), which today, unfortunately for the Prado, are treasured in the collections of other countries. *Diana and Actaeon* and its pendant, *Diana and Callisto,* today in the collection at Bridgewater House, London, were given by Philip V to the Duc d'Orléans. He also gave away the magnificent *Rape of Europa* now in the Isabella Stewart Gardner collection in Boston. The Louvre's *Jupiter and Antiope* was presented by Philip IV to Prince Charles, later King Charles I, of England, and finally the beautiful late work *Tarquin and Lucretia* was carried off by Joseph Bonaparte during the Peninsular War and found its way eventually to the Fitzwilliam Museum in Cambridge. If we are to accept as literally true Titian's begging letter of February, 1576, to Philip, the old painter was never paid for the pictures supplied to Spain since the death of Charles V.

At about the middle point in Philip II's reign, which lasted from 1556 to 1598, there occurred in Spanish cultural life a strange and important event —or rather advent: the arrival of Domenicos Theotocopoulos, the Byzantine painter from Crete (born 1541). He had gone to Venice at about the age of twenty-five when Crete, still a dependency of that powerful city-state, was in immediate danger of falling to the Turks, as Naxos and Chios had recently fallen. In Venice the young Cretan, who was soon known simply as "The Greek" (Il Greco or El Greco) became a pupil of the aging Titian, and also was influenced by the more agitated figure compositions of Tintoretto and Jacopo Bassano. In 1570, armed with introductions from the miniaturist Giulio Clovio, he had gone to Rome with the intention of studying the sculptures and paintings of Michelangelo. In the time of his Roman sojourn he must have painted the version of *The Expulsion from the Temple* now in Minneapolis. In its lower right corner appear four portraits. Three reproduce the familiar features of Titian, Michelangelo, and Giulio Clovio. The fourth shows a long-haired younger man, evidently between thirty and forty years old, and of strong personality. He has heavy features, and his burning eyes are directed at the beholder, while his index finger points significantly at himself. It is El Greco himself, *se ipse pinxit*, according to the argument of Edgar Wind, and the only acceptable portrait of him.

Exactly when this long-haired El Greco reached Spain is not known. It was probably in or about 1575, for his important retable painted for the Toledan church of Santo Domingo el Antiguo bears the date 1577. The uppermost picture from this complex, *The Holy Trinity*, is now in the Prado (plate 17). Philip ordered two paintings from El Greco for the Escorial where they are still preserved, the strange *Dream of Philip II*, recalling Titian's *Gloria* painted for Charles V, and *The Martyrdom of St. Maurice and His Theban Legion*, a large and brilliantly conceived work. But Philip did not really care for El Greco's painting. In developing his strongly individual style, so perfectly suited to the expression of his own passionate mysticism, El Greco had already traveled so far from the Venetian modes to which Philip had given his allegiance that there was no keeping pace with him. Fortunately the churches and convents in Toledo and elsewhere gave the Greek as much patronage as he could accept, recognizing perhaps unconsciously that he expressed more perfectly than any native Spaniard was able to, the religious enthusiasms of Spain in a century when Ignatius Loyola and Theresa of Avila flourished. And it was from the religious foundations, suppressed in 1835, that most of the Prado's El Grecos came. None came from Philip II.

A PAINTER ESPECIALLY FAVORED by Philip was Hieronymus Bosch, the North Netherlandish painter of *diableries*. Just how many of Bosch's works Philip owned nobody knows, but he must have had more than anyone else before or since; perhaps he had 36 as one scholar believed. He obtained them from various sources. A few he inherited from Charles V, who was sixteen years old in 1516, the year in which Bosch died. Indeed Charles could well have known Bosch personally, for the distance between Malines, where Charles lived, and 's-Hertogenbosch, the home of Bosch, is less than eighty miles. Six Bosches Philip bought from the widow and son of Felipe de Guevara, a courtier of Emperor Charles and the author of *Commentarios de la Pintura*. The Epiphany triptych (plate 112), Bosch's masterpiece in the opinion of Max J. Friedländer, was confiscated by Philip from a certain rebellious Netherlandish burgher. But on the debit side, at least four Bosches are thought to have been lost when the Pardo Palace burned in 1604, and others almost certainly were burned in the Alcázar fire in 1734. The superlative triptych with *The Temptation of Saint Anthony*, now in the Lisbon Museum, is thought to have left Spain as a gift from the Spanish royal family. The works by this bizarre painter which have survived in Spain were probably among the 13 which Philip sent to the Escorial in 1574. His craze for these fantastic masterpieces seems to have caused some of his subjects a great deal of concern, and José de Sigüenza, for one, understandably in dread of the very active Inquisition, wrote an elaborate argument directing attention to the fidelity to nature and the intrinsic orthodoxy of Bosch's pictures.

In his enthusiasm for Bosch, Philip II evidenced a taste as independent as it was sound, and the admirable perspicuity which he showed in that instance he showed again in his effective interest in the somewhat younger Netherlander, Joachim de Patinir. The four landscapes in the Prado (see plates 87, 88 & 95) and the one at El Escorial were probably all acquired by Philip. The groups of figures illustrating stories, Christian or pagan, are mere excuses for Patinir's unrolling of the wondrous expansive countryside which they inhabit; and as the writer Carel van Mander (1604) observed, the figures were even in some instances painted by collaborative artists, such as Quentin Massys and Joos van Cleve.

Aside from his activity in connection with art

and the Escorial, Philip II devoted himself with unresting zeal to his duties as King of Spain. A portrait of him by Mor painted in 1550, when Philip was twenty-three, shows a young person of unusual charm and good looks. Another handsome portrait of him, the full-length one in armor painted by Titian in 1551, was sent by Philip's aunt, Maria of Hungary, to Mary of England, Philip's thirty-eight-year-old fiancée. The marriage, an affair of state, was a dutiful act indeed on Philip's part. He built for Mary a palace in Norman style in the park of the Buen Retiro, but she never reached Spain. She died four years after the marriage and left no progeny. There was some talk then of a marriage with Queen Elizabeth, but she avoided it, and when, thirty years later, in 1588, she sent troops to help the Protestant princes on the continent, Philip sought to punish her once and forever by dispatching the "Invincible Armada" against England. After the defeat, Philip regretted sadly that he had been "unable to render God this great service," protesting that after all he had never sent his fleet to defeat the weather. The disastrous results for Spanish wealth and power more than wiped out the glory of the naval victory which had been gained against the Turks seventeen years earlier at Lepanto, in which the combined fleets of Spain, Venice, and the Pope had been led by Don Juan of Austria, a gallant natural son of Charles V.

IN THE LOW COUNTRIES the troubles of Spain increased. The Regent, Margaret of Parma, the daughter of Charles V by a Flemish lady, and the widow of Ottavio Farnese, was unable or unwilling to take the drastic measures required to suppress the growing popular revolt, and Philip in 1567 sent the harsh Duke of Alba with seasoned Spanish troops. The brutality and oppressiveness of this regime only strengthened the resolution of the Protestant Netherlanders to achieve independence, and Alba was replaced by more diplomatic rulers. In 1584 Philip procured the assassination of William the Silent, and finally in 1598, not long before he died, he ceded the "Spanish Netherlands" to his daughter Isabella Clara Eugenia as a sort of dowry upon her marriage with Archduke Albert of Austria. The struggle to control the Netherlands continued for another fifty years, until the Peace of Westphalia in 1648 marked a positive conclusion to Spanish

rule there and gave religious liberty to the Northern provinces.

In 1580 Philip went to great lengths in the employment of force and trickery in order to annex to Spain the kingdom of Portugal where the throne had become vacant. When his purpose was achieved (not permanently, as it turned out) he wisely allowed the Portuguese almost complete autonomy, for he was indeed a complex character. His niece Anna of Austria, whom he had married ten years before as his fourth wife, died at Badajoz in Estremadura near the Portuguese frontier when she accompanied him on his journey to take possession of the new land. From Lisbon a few months later Philip wrote a letter to his and Anna's two daughters expressing regret that they had not been with him to see the Corpus Christi procession there, "although," he added, "your little brother if he were along might have been frightened of some devils which resembled those in paintings by Hieronymus Bosch."

In 1574, long before the building of the Escorial was completed, Philip had moved thither many of his favorite religious paintings. He himself, disheartened by the death of his wife, moved into an austere cell-like room where from his bed he could look down upon the high altar of the monastery church. It was there that he died at the age of seventy-one, securely mindful of the fact that directly beneath the high altar the gloomy royal burial chamber would soon be provided.

Philip III, who reigned from 1598 to 1621, was the son of Philip II by his fourth wife, Anna of Austria; indeed, it was to him (then three years old) that his father referred in the letter from Lisbon to the two young princesses, mentioning the Corpus Christi procession. The new Philip, who became King at the age of twenty, cared more for hunting than for art. Indeed, his views on art were cynical and philistine. It was early in his reign that the Pardo fire occurred in which so many fine paintings were destroyed, and after the repairs to the building had been made, Philip seemed satisfied to replace Titians and Mors with portraits by the mundane Pantoja de la Cruz and the obscure Bartolomé González, declaring that nobody would perceive the difference. It was about one year before the fire that Philip and his influential minister, the Duke of Lerma, received a ceremonial visit of several months from Rubens, then aged twenty-six, who came on a diplomatic mission from the Duke of Mantua. Then it was that Rubens painted the somewhat diffuse equestrian portrait of the Duke of Lerma, now in the Kunsthistorisches Museum at Vienna. He also painted for Lerma pictures of Heraclitus and Democritus, and the set of half-length apostles, most of which came much later into the possession of the Prado. Philip III and the Duke of Lerma are, however, best remembered for their expulsion from Spain of the subject Moorish inhabitants, the *Moriscos*. These Arabs and Berbers who had remained after the Reconquest constituted the thriftiest and most industrious element of the population, to whom much credit must be given for Spain's enormous production of exportable fine wool and manufactured cloth as well as silk, both raw and fabricated. Historians estimate that the *Moriscos* expelled in the time of Philip III may have numbered as many as half a million. The Edict of 1567, in Philip II's time, had already left much agricultural land in a state of vacancy and neglect, and this new wave of intolerance made matters far worse for agriculture and also for the spinning and weaving industries. The weakening effect on Spain was similar to that which the revocation of the Edict of Nantes, aimed against the Protestant Huguenots in France, was to have in that country a generation or two later.

Despite the long succession of royal extravagances and blunders, the costly struggle for European religious unity, the wars for territorial aggrandizement, and the wholesale expulsion of productive workers, Spain remained for some time longer one of the great European powers—perhaps the greatest, thanks largely to the continued importation from the American colonies of an enormous wealth in commodities as well as in precious metals. In America the Spanish fleet and soldiery were in general successful in fighting off English and Dutch expansionism.

THE NEW KING, Philip IV, who reigned from 1621 to 1665, celebrated some of the victories in this colonial warfare and added others from the Thirty Years War in Europe by commissioning a series of paintings of them as large as ten feet by twelve. These works and more besides were in their places on the walls of the Hall of Kingdoms in the Buen Retiro palace at the time of its formal opening in 1635. Philip IV as a youth, and increasingly as he grew to maturity, was a person of sophistication and wide culture, a good linguist, a producer of amateur theatricals, and even a serious practitioner of the art of painting. His devotion to these pursuits caused him inevitably to delegate much of his royal power to his Minister, the Count-Duke of Olivares, whose services he had inherited from his father. On the other hand, his fine connoisseurship and ample income, in auspicious conjunction with the ascendant and supreme painters, Velázquez and Rubens, made it possible for him to be one of the greatest collectors, if not *the* greatest, in European history.

Of about 48 to 50 works by Velázquez in the Prado (critics are not quite agreed), some 40 were owned originally by Philip IV himself. The only other important group, that in Vienna, consists of five or six brilliant portraits of members of the Spanish branch of the Hapsburgs which were sent by Philip to the Austrian branch, perhaps merely as a kinsman's reports on the rising generation but more likely as tempting bait which could lead to new intra-familial marriages. Contrary to earlier opinions, however, Velázquez painted a considerable number of pictures for people other than the royal family. He preserved his aristocratic dignity by consistently refusing payment. Somewhat as in the case of Rembrandt with his busy workshop, Velázquez with his son-in-law Mazo and perhaps others to help him left many problems for the perplexity of scholars. The total count of the surviving paintings which may be considered to be by his own hand is one which depends on the connoisseurship and temperament of the individual scholar. Beruete accepted less than 100; Allende-Salazar 114; Lafuente 122; Trapier 80; and Ortega y Gasset 86. The list made by A. L. Mayer, containing as it does numerous frankly questionable works and many more which are *somewhat* questionable, is not easily counted but surely reaches into the hundreds.

Don Diego Velázquez de Silva was born in 1599 of a good *hidalgo* family in the important commercial port city of Seville. There he studied art under Pacheco, a pedantic but respected painter, a writer on art, and the artistic advisor to the Inquisition. At the age of twenty-one Velázquez had already become an impressive painter of portraits and of the genre pictures called *bodegones*, which showed simple folk working or eating in kitchens or in modest inns. He painted in a strong chiaroscuro suggesting the indirect influence of Caravaggio, although some writers on matters of art think that painting in strong light and shade was simply "in the air" as an expression of the generally emphatic temper of the period.

When Velázquez reached the age of about twenty-three, the King's minister Olivares, himself a Sevillian, brought him to Madrid. His personality and his painting pleased the young King from the first, and he remained in the royal service for the rest of his life, developing himself gradually into one of the very great painters, partly through his unsurpassed subtlety in enveloping his subjects in light and air. He was temperamentally a pantheist, giving equal value and importance to whatever he painted, whether king or dwarf or dog. Havelock Ellis describes a parallel to Velázquez' art when he characterizes Spanish dancing with its extraordinary intensity as being "saved from lawlessness by the instinctive dignity and self-respect of the Spaniard and his profound love of decorum and beautiful ritual." In the Spanish dance, which is the symbolized representation of the drama of love, the dancers advance, recede, and eddy about one another, effectively heightening the tension by their strict renunciation of physical contact. It is in the bullfight that the Spaniard achieves the ultimate climax of such controlled and stylized action. However that may be, the quality of genius under dignified restraint in this youthful Sevillian caused his royal employer to treat him with "incredible affability," to use the proud expression of Velázquez' father-in-law Pacheco. Velázquez had been assigned a large apartment in the Alcázar, the old royal palace, and Pacheco reported that "the King had a key to the artist's studio and a chair of his own there in order to watch Velázquez painting almost every day."

An important ingredient in Velázquez's development, and of Philip's as well, must have been the second visit of Rubens to the Spanish court. His first, in 1603, had occurred before Philip IV was born and now, in 1628–29, for more than half a year he was abundantly present, having been sent on a sort of political errand by his patroness, the Infanta Isabel Clara Eugenia, daughter of Philip II and ruler of the Netherlands. For her he had just completed the set of 17 paintings to be woven as tapestries, with subjects celebrating the Church and the Eucharist. Eight of these are now in the Prado (see plate 127).

The famous Flemish painter and man of the world, old enough to be the father of Philip or Velázquez, wrote home to his friend Peiresc that he had been seeing the Spanish King a great deal and found that he possessed excellent qualities, including an unmistakable taste for paintings. Rubens must have seen a great deal of Velázquez too, and together they looked at the paintings in the Alcázar and also journeyed out to the Escorial. A few years before the visit of Rubens, Philip had bought at an auction Rubens' important *Adoration of the Magi*, painted in 1609, and Rubens took the opportunity of his stay in Madrid to enlarge it and to repaint it extensively. Also he made for himself full-scale copies of many of the Titians in the royal collections. At least two of these Philip bought later from the Rubens estate (see plate 121).

The personal connection between the Flemish painter and Philip was mutually advantageous in bringing to the royal collection some years later 112 canvases by Rubens, mostly painted in the free and impassioned style of his last period, between 1636 and 1638. A few of these works were painted in collaboration with helpers in his workshop, and a few others were made by well-known Antwerp artists basing their paintings on the master's oil sketches. From the lot, many were commissioned for the Torre de la Parada, where, unfortunately, they were subjected to terrible looting and destruction in 1710 when Austrian, Dutch, and English troops ran wild in Madrid during the War of the Spanish Succession. However, the remaining pictures, mostly based on subjects from Ovid's *Metamorphoses*, constitute one of the prime contributions to the present-day glory of the Prado.

A more immediate consequence of Rubens' visit to Madrid was the prompt departure of Velázquez on a visit of more than a year in Italy, his first journey there; for it is safe to assume that the King was moved to grant the leave of absence by the persuasion of the Flemish master, whose own art had profited so much from his long stay in Italy. Before he left Spain, Velázquez had painted the spirited and realistic *Triumph of Bacchus*, known as *The Topers (Los Borrachos;* plate 25); and when he came back he brought with him two more such historical-mythological subjects which he had painted in Italy. These reveal a decidedly lighter touch. This lighter, looser, and thinner way of painting he was to develop continuously in his portraits of the royal personages and their dwarfs and *locos*. Elizabeth du Gué Trapier quotes a Spanish writer, Andrés de Uztárroz, who in 1646 praises Velázquez' "subtle skill which with a few strokes show how much art, freedom of touch, and rapid execution can accomplish."

IN JANUARY, 1649, Velázquez began a second journey to Italy. Much of his time there was to be spent in buying, or attempting to buy, paintings and sculptures for Philip. But also he painted two unique small views of the gardens at the Villa Medici in Rome (see plate 30), precursors of Corot's views of the Eternal City. In addition, he made a number of portraits, including the penetrating likeness of the ruddy and dangerous-looking Pope Innocent X, now in the Doria-Pamphili Gallery, Rome—a portrait considered by many to be one of the world's greatest. In February, 1650, the King wrote to his ambassador in Rome directing him to see that Velázquez' "phlegmatic temperament" should not prevent his returning to Madrid by the first of June at the latest. Despite his gratifying sympathy for art, Philip with his strictures about Velázquez' slow pace could hardly have been aware of the epochal innovations in the art of painting over which he had seen his First Painter deliberating. In any case, Velázquez was enormously interested in the things he was seeing and the people he was meeting in Italy, and it was a full year later than Philip's deadline before he reached Madrid. He had been directed to bring with him to Spain the famous Italian painter-decorator, Pietro (Berretini) da Cortona, but Pietro declined the invitation.

The last decade of Velázquez' life brought forth paintings in which his ultimate aims were best achieved: the shimmering portraits of the new Queen and of the royal children, and the two inexhaustible pictures, *The Maids of Honor* (plate 31) and *The Spinners* (plate 32), in which the diverse personages are revealed as though casually in a veritable bath of subtle lighting and vibrating atmosphere.

But Philip's acquisitions did not end with the works of Velázquez and Rubens. To mention a few, he added importantly to the collections of Titians (see plates 138 and 139) already intelligently begun by the Emperor Charles and methodically amplified by Philip II; he made purchases of pictures by Tintoretto (plates 154–157), mostly negotiated by Velázquez; and also he bought several wonderful Veroneses (see plate 158). It was he who bought the Prado's group of paintings by Raphael

(see plates 137 & 144), some of them, on high authority, executed partly by his assistants, but scarcely less fine for that. A set of four lyrical landscapes by Claude (see plates 163 & 164) were commissioned from the artist himself by Philip's ambassador in Rome. From the sale of the effects of Charles I of England after his execution, Philip acquired the rare little Mantegna now in the Prado (plate 135) and the youthful self-portrait of Albrecht Dürer (plate 96). The two panels by the same master illustrating *Adam and Eve* (plate 97) were a gift to Philip from Queen Christine of Sweden. In the leading contemporary Spanish painters other than Velázquez, Philip IV showed little or no interest. He possessed nothing by Murillo, and the only Zurbaráns he acquired were the comparatively unimpressive examples which he had ordered for the Hall of Kingdoms. A few fine paintings by Ribera he may have had, such as the vigorous *Martyrdom of Saint Bartholomew* (plate 23), for several of Philip's successive viceroys at Naples, where Ribera worked, were lovers of art and brought his paintings back to Spain.

Isabelle of France, whom Philip IV had married in his youth, died in 1644, and a few years later he imported his niece Mariana of Austria, who was to have married his young son, Prince Baltasar Carlos. But the Prince died even before the arrival of the bride-to-be, and Philip himself married her when she reached the age of fifteen. She was the mother of Philip's heir, Charles II, known in Spain as *Carlos el Hechizado* ("the Bewitched") because of his dim intelligence. With his mental incapacity and his extreme youth at the time of his father's death in 1665, his reign of thirty-five years led to the regency of the Queen Mother, not famous for ability, and later encouraged the scheming of ministers who were at liberty to mismanage his—and Spain's—affairs. Politically it was a depressing and demoralizing period, and royal art acquisitions languished too. Carreño de Miranda was a poor successor to Velázquez as court portraitist (see plate 53), and Luca Giordano, brought from Italy in 1692, deserved all too well his nickname *Fa Presto* or "He Does It Quick." Charles the Bewitched died without issue, the last of the Spanish Hapsburgs. Much to the point is Hume's summary of that dynasty: "From the greatest Charles to the smallest one, disaster and decay had pursued their unfortunate people." It had been a period of less than two centuries, from 1516 to 1700.

Feeble of understanding though he unquestionably was, *El Hechizado* on his deathbed was able to indicate his royal choice as to his successor, and his choice was law. His French courtiers had won against the Austrian clique, and Philip of Anjou, a grandson of Louis XIV, became King of Spain as Philip V. Yet the exhausting War of the Spanish Succession still had to be fought to make his throne secure, for there were European powers that feared the results if the Bourbons were to rule in Spain as well as in France. It was in 1710 during the effort of the combined troops of England, Austria, and Holland to unseat Philip V that the deplorable looting of Madrid occurred, and no part of the city suffered more cruelly that the Torre de la Parada with its irreplaceable art. In 1734, still during the reign of Philip, the terrible Christmas Eve conflagration took place. This time it was in the Alcázar, destroying the palace completely along with who knows how many of its paintings. The royal family was not in residence there at that moment, and if the flames in fact spread as fast as the Christmas revellers later testified, the wonder is that so many paintings were saved.

In 1714, twenty years before the fire, Philip V had married his second wife, the forceful Elisabetta (or Isabella) Farnese, daughter of the Duke of Parma; and after that dreadful Christmas the royal pair promptly set about planning the splendid new Royal Palace on the bluff above the Manzanares River, the site of the palace that had burned down. It was not completed, however, until 1764, in the reign of Charles III. Both Philip the Bourbon and Isabella Farnese had grown up in families habituated to art collecting, and they inherited their families' enthusiasms, though apparently inheriting few of the actual works of art. To a large extent their collections, now in the Prado, were made and owned separately. Early in their reign they maintained the Court at Seville for some time, and it was during this residence that Isabella "discovered" Murillo, who despite the admirable qualities of his painting had been as little favored by Philip IV as he is in many quarters today. While there in Murillo's own beguiling Andalusian metropolis, the Queen bought 29 paintings by him, and judging by the 11 of them which may be seen in the Prado (see plates 54, 55 & 57), her selection could scarcely have been better. The circumstance that the number of Murillos now existing is so small a fraction of those in Isabella's original purchase may be due to the oc-

currence in 1748 of yet another fire in the palace at Aranjuez, which had suffered similar catastrophes in 1660 and 1665.

I SABELLA FARNESE'S INTEREST IN PAINTINGS was avid and remarkably inclusive. To her collection the Prado owes two outstanding works by Jordaens (see plate 130), a pair of elegant, small Watteaus—the only ones in the Museum (plates 165 & 166), several fine Van Dycks, a beautiful Veronese, and two portraits by Velázquez, one being the so-called *Sibyl,* thought to be a likeness of the artist's wife, Juana Pacheco. Isabella had also acquired works by Ribera, including one of his most startlingly naturalistic and stirring pictures, *Jacob's Dream* (plate 10). Besides seizing upon such incontestably important paintings as these, the enthusiasm of *La Farnesio* extended to the works of a wide variety of enjoyable lesser artists. She possessed between twenty and thirty pictures by Teniers, father and son, perhaps a dozen by Wouvermans, three landscapes by Lucas van Valckenborch, some typical pictures of dead birds by Jan Fyt, a sulky alleged self-portrait by Artemisia Gentileschi (plate 149), and paintings by Jan Brueghel, Guercino, and many others. Much of the time of Philip V and his Queen was spent at La Granja, and there they kept most of their paintings. They built this palace at San Ildefonso near Segovia, and designed it in the French style of the time, with formal gardens reminiscent of Versailles. The royal pair also spent some of their time at Aranjuez, south of Madrid, where they had restored the old palace.

Philip V, as a son of the Grand Dauphin, Louis de France, had inherited from him a famous collection of objects carved from semi-precious stones, which is now in the Prado. Most of his paintings, on the other hand, appear to have been bought personally, and although Isabella too seems to have followed this practice in her collecting, it is probable that many of their purchases were made jointly. Of the paintings in the Prado which are marked as from Philip's own collection at La Granja, a group of nine by Poussin demands the most enthusiastic praise. Especially is this true of the picture of young David after his triumph over Goliath (plate 161), which a leading Italian critic has characterized as "sublime," and also of the noble, classical scene on Mount Parnassus with its numerous muses, poets, and philosophers happily disposed upon its flank (plate 162). By Poussin there are landscapes too in the collection, and five in addition by Gaspard Dughet, his brother-in-law. Further there is one landscape each by Annibale Carracci and Claude Lorrain, and one portrait each by Largillière and Rigaud. In addition to his excellent paintings by French artists, Philip—perhaps in his desire further to allay homesickness—imported court portraitists from France. They were capable technicians but devoid of any sparks of genius. Jean Ranc, for one, arrived in Madrid in 1724 and recorded on a series of canvases the appearance of members of the Spanish Bourbon family. In 1743 they were again placed on record, this time by Louis Michel van Loo, and all on a single canvas thirteen feet high and sixteen feet wide.

Among the younger personages portrayed have been identified the Infantes Charles (born in 1716) and Philip (born in 1720), both of them sons of Philip V and Isabella Farnese. But the heir apparent to the Spanish throne was Ferdinand, the son of Philip by his former wife, and as this inevitable fact bored in, Isabella became as restless as a she-bear in springtime. Thrones simply must be found for her own two cubs, and the quest for these thrones involved the Spanish people once again in warfare, just at a time when Philip's famous minister, the Marqués de la Ensenada, seemed to be getting the country into a more coordinated and prosperous state. In the end, while Philip V lay prostrated by melancholia, the thrones were produced. Charles was to have the kingdom of the Two Sicilies when its throne became vacant, and young Philip, who had been given in marriage to a daughter of Louis XV of France, was later promised the dukedom of Parma.

On July 9, 1746, Philip V suddenly died, perhaps more worn out by peace conferences than by wars. As anticipated, he was succeeded by his first wife's son, who now became King of Spain as Ferdinand VI. Fortunate is the country that has no history, as the saying goes, and the uneventful reign of Ferdinand VI, though only thirteen years long, gave Spain a badly needed interlude during which to recover her balance (partly achieved already in Philip V's reign despite the wars), and to revive to some extent her production of essential goods. As to the interim condition of the art of painting, it was in abeyance so far as native painters were concerned, and the Court, to fill the gap, sent to Italy for the painters Amigoni and Giaquinto, for there were still empty ceilings and walls to be painted in the new Royal Palace and also in the Escorial, at Buen Retiro, and at Aranjuez. Smaller paintings by Giaquinto are in the Prado, and an interesting recent purchase is the portrait by Amigoni of Ferdinand's minister, the Marqués de la Ensenada.

Isabella Farnese survived her husband by twenty years, and she also survived his son Ferdinand. Thus she had the satisfaction of seeing her child, whom she had long since maneuvered onto the throne at Naples, elevated in 1759 to the more exalted throne of Spain, as Charles III. The nineteen years he had spent in a large non-Iberian city seem to have had a liberalizing effect upon his ideas concerning a monarch's duties, just as a Parisian upbringing had affected Philip V. Thus the reign of Charles III was one which encouraged the academies of the arts and sciences. It will be remembered that the building used for the Museo del Prado was built originally by Charles III as a science museum. During his reign noble attempts were made to improve agriculture and industry. New and less cordial relations were established with the Church, which had opposed the Bourbon rule in Spain, and with the Inquisition, the severity of which had come to seem too outmoded. The Jesuits, who were considered by the King to have overplayed their hand, were actually expelled—although later under Ferdinand VII they were back again.

Charles was much interested in sponsoring the minor arts and established a fine porcelain factory at Buen Retiro in Madrid. Also he gave encouragement to tapestry weaving at the Santa Bárbara factory. He had been enthusiastic over classical art when still in Naples, and in 1761 brought to Spain the classicist Bohemian painter Anton Rafael Mengs, who soon became the totalitarian art dictator there, much as David was to be in France a generation later. Mengs became also the Director of the Academy of the Fine Arts of San Fernando, which had recently been founded. His advice was everywhere considered invaluable, and the King was wise in accepting it when it led to his acquiring Pieter Bruegel's *Triumph of Death* (plate 117), and Velázquez's *Portrait of the Count-Duke of Olivares on Horseback*. Soon after Meng's arrival at the court came the great Venetian, Giovanni Battista Tiepolo, accompanied by his two sons, to paint ceilings in the new palace. The ceiling of the huge Throne Room, painted by Tiepolo, must have had an important influence on other painters in

Madrid. There in the Royal Palace could be seen as clearly as anywhere in Europe the opposition which the new, smooth, competent academicians represented by Mengs offered to the baroque and rococo styles of such painters as Giaquinto and Tiepolo.

As the King's director of art, Mengs was in charge of the Santa Bárbara tapestry factory, and in that capacity showed a surprisingly flexible policy, involving the displacement of the customary regurgitated and reworked themes of Teniers and Wouvermans with subjects from the popular daily activities and pastimes (perhaps a little freshened and sweetened?) of contemporary Spanish people. To paint the cartoons he chose as his chief artist Francisco Bayeu of Saragossa. And that pointed the way for the career of Francisco Goya, the most various and spirited genius in the rich history of Spanish painting.

GOYA WAS BORN IN 1746 AT FUENDETODOS, an Aragonese village too small and miserable to be mentioned by Baedeker in our time, and equally negligible in the eighteenth century. He was apprenticed to a little-known painter, and later in nearby Saragossa he came to know and work under Bayeu, whose sister he soon married. Somehow about 1770–71 he managed a trip to Italy, and it seems not unlikely that he saw the Tiepolo decorations at Villa Valmarana in Vicenza, for his work on tapestry cartoons later was far more like these than like the formal work which Tiepolo executed in the Royal Palace and elsewhere in Madrid.

When he was twenty-nine, Goya joined the staff at the tapestry factory, and between 1775 and 1792 received payment for 63 cartoons for tapestries, painted at full scale and in oil on canvas. Goya's style was not yet quite his own, and thus some of the cartoons painted as early as 1775, such as the *Boar Hunt* and *Dogs with Hunting Gear*, were thought until recently to be by Francisco Bayeu's younger brother, Ramón, but the thorough study which Don V. de Sambricio has given to the factory records proves that these two are by Goya. By August, 1777, two years later, Goya already had developed a style far finer in its color and drawing and much broader in its humanity than the other designers were capable of, and thus the possibility of further misattribution is eliminated. The cartoons, rolled into bundles and forgotten in the basement of the Royal Palace, were rescued about 1870

by Federico de Madrazo, and 44 by Goya are now in the Prado (see plates 59 & 66), while two more are lent from there to one of the government buildings. The same qualities of true observation and effective technical freedom, when applied by Goya to portraits, resulted in some of the most enjoyable portraits aesthetically, and at the same time the most penetrating psychologically, to be found anywhere. Goya was too proud and too sturdily honest to dilute the truths which his eyes could see, and whatever he saw his fluent brush knew how to give expression to. His work is as free from the ironic exaggeration, often imputed to him, as from polite fibbing. Probably no civilization has produced an equally observant and brilliant pictorial reporter. He seems always to be saying, "This is exactly what they looked like."

Goya lived far beyond the reign of Charles III, which ended in 1788, and he was continued as Court Painter by Charles' affable and ineffectual forty-year-old son, Charles IV. This fourth Charles continued to be known as the King of Spain for twenty years, although he preferred to leave affairs of state to the management of his outrageous Queen, María Luisa of Parma, and her lover the Chief Minister Godoy. These people, and others of the sort, Goya portrayed. His earlier portraits, painted within the eighteenth century, still have much of the courtly rococo look about them, but no painter was earlier than Goya in arriving at the full grasp of the nineteenth century, with its informal spirit and its impressionistic technique.

At the age of forty-six Goya had a severe illness which left him stone deaf, and after that he may have read more and thought more, but his letters were never those of a man of culture. However, his candor, his vitality, his restless curiosity about the nature of his fellow-man, and with it all his pithy up-country speech, of which we gain a clear idea from the short-cut remarks he scribbled on many of his drawings—all of this, where his friends were concerned, must have gone far indeed toward making up for his loss of hearing. It was not long after the onset of his deafness that Goya found himself in the midst of his famous (though always somewhat conjectural) love affair with the spirited and capricious Duchess of Alba. Evidently they went to her estate in Andalusia, but how did they converse—or were both of them a little weary of the gabble of Madrid?

Another question persistently arising concerns

the witches that appear in Goya's drawings and prints with such immediacy and conviction that they seem to have been personally experienced. Did Goya, at least halfway, believe in them? Some scholars answer with an indignant negative. But perhaps these are overmodernized. Experts report on encounters with witches near Goya's old village as late as the beginning of the twentieth century, and the authoritative (though not official) Catholic Encyclopedia warns of "the undeniable possibility of a diabolical interference in human affairs." Charles Poore, in his readable book about Goya, thinks that the hair-raising apparitions of Goya's childhood in Fuendetodos haunted him all his life, adding, "He spoke out against the ignorance that bred these superstitions, yet one wonders . . ."

But everyone knows about Goya, the youthful matador, the great painter, the privileged lover, the self-exiled liberal! At the Prado one finds not only his great paintings, but also numerous fascinating drawings, which might be called incomparable except for those of Rembrandt. The Prado also offers the visitor the entire set of brooding nightmares painted by Goya in his seventies directly on the walls of his little country house, the *Quinta del Sordo* or "Deaf Man's House" (see plate 49). But these and some others came to the Prado later than the reign of Charles IV. However, Charles should doubtless be given credit for supplying the pictures made by his own Court Painter. He also made a few fine purchases. The Prado's beautiful altarwings by Robert Campin (plate 90), identified by many with the Master of Flémalle, were bought by Charles, and he bought also the sensitive *Portrait of a Cardinal* by Raphael (plate 136)—though under the impression that he was acquiring a painting by Anthonis Mor!

I N THE FATEFUL YEAR 1808 Napoleon cast his covetous eyes toward Spain. He found it easy to bamboozle both Charles and his son Ferdinand VII into surrendering the Spanish throne to his brother Joseph Bonaparte, for both of these Bourbons had evil in their own hearts, and such people are said to make the easiest victims for confidence men. The Spanish people as a whole rose up in brave resistance, but even with Wellington's help it took them four years to drive the French usurper back across the Pyrenees. Two stirring paintings by Goya (plates 71 & 72) celebrate the initial resistance of the people and the bloody reprisal of the invader.

Ferdinand VII, who had spent the difficult years of the invasion as a prisoner in France, now returned to his throne. But his reactionary rule drove out many of the Spanish liberals, who found refuge in France, especially in Bordeaux. There in 1824 old Goya joined them to spend enjoyably and productively the last years of his life. Back in Spain, Ferdinand VII had to be forced by the revolt of the army before he was prepared to agree to the liberal Constitution of 1812. But the old Hapsburg-Bourbon tradition of art collecting still activated him occasionally, and the Prado Museum is indebted to him for his purchase of two fine Zurbaráns celebrating St. Peter Nolasco (plates 24 & 33) as well as El Greco's *Holy Trinity* (plate 17), Velázquez' *Christ on the Cross,* and three Riberas. Ferdinand VII was the last of the royal collectors of Spain but (when his politics are disregarded) is recognized and remembered rather as the official founder of the Prado Museum.

Earlier in this Introduction, the observation was made that the changing in 1868 of the name of the institution from the *Real Museo* to the *Museo del Prado* was accompanied by a substantial alteration in its general status. The royal family ceased giving its private financial support and patronage, and the responsibility passed to the State and later to the *Patronato* or Board of Directors, a more accessible situation which permitted private owners of fine paintings to feel more friendly, more involved with the collection.

One of the first important increments to the collection under the new status was the large group of drawings by Goya which came to the Prado in 1866; a second lot came twenty years later. Most of them had belonged to Valentín Carderera, a profound admirer of Goya. Another great accession of Goya's work consisted in the gift from Baron Emile d'Erlanger, a Swiss, of the 14 terrifying frescoes removed, as noted above, from the walls of Goya's *Quinta.* Mention should be made also of the transfer to the Prado in 1872 of the contents of the Trinidad Museum in Madrid, which had been founded in 1835–36 to house paintings expropriated from recently secularized convents. The Trinidad collection had occasionally been enriched by the Crown, and the Prado received 84 paintings, not counting the modern ones which were bestowed on other institutions. The bequest of Pablo Bosch in 1915 brought another varied lot of paintings, which included the lovely *Rest on the Flight into Egypt* by Gerard David (plate 85), the exceptionally perfect *Virgin and Child* by the mystical painter Morales (plate 7), and two works by El Greco.

The bequest of Fernández-Durán in 1930 was one of the most important. It included tapestries and other fine decorative objects, but especially the excellent *Virgin and Child* (plate 92) by Rogier van der Weyden, the frightening *Colossus* by Goya (plate 63), a fine portrait also by him, together with several delightful small paintings based on his style in the tapestry cartoons. The year 1930 was marked also by the acceptance of a fund from the Conde de Cartagena from which have been made a number of admirable purchases, such as Zurbarán's *St. Luke Painting the Crucified Christ* (plate 35), Scorel's *Portrait of a Humanist* (plate 99), Mazo's *Stag Hunt*, and Ribalta's *The Crucified Christ Embracing St. Bernard*. More recently there came from the Conde de Mugiro the two strikingly vital and modern pictures which Goya painted in Bordeaux in 1827 and 1828 (?), the last years of his life (see plate 73). In 1952 through an accord with the Kress Foundation in the United States came four panels by Juan de Flandes, characterized in the Prado catalogue as "most beautiful" (*hermosisimas*).

Further purchases have been made by the Prado through its Board and through the National Ministry of Education. These include Van der Weyden's *Pietà* (plate 75), the fifteenth-century Hispano-Flemish *Archangel Michael* (plate 1), works by Yáñez de la Almedina (including his lovely *St. Catherine*, plate 5), Bermejo's majestic portrait of the enthroned Santo Domingo de Silos (plate 2), and the portrait of the Marqués de la Ensenada, painted by Amigoni. The tendency is evidently to fill the gaps and balance the collection.

The Civil War in 1936 placed the contents of the Prado in imminent danger of destruction. The Museum staff with great skill and enterprise removed hundreds of the greatest paintings to one place after another that seemed to promise security—and in the end saved everything.

In the past few years the Spanish government has benefited tourists and art lovers in Madrid by transferring to the Prado (for how long one cannot tell) masterpieces from the Escorial, such as *The Descent from the Cross* by Rogier van der Weyden (plate 91) and *The Garden of Delights* by Hieronymus Bosch (plate 106).

In 1912, when the Board of Directors was established by royal decree, the pious hope was expressed that the Prado Museum would cease to be a "splendid but irregular" picture collection and become a properly organized museum. With her sensitive appreciation of the Prado's present emphasis on a comparatively few artists whose work had appealed especially to the monarchs, Enriqueta Harris, in her account of the Prado, frankly rejoices in the "splendid but irregular" proportioning of the collection and delights in her confidence that it can never become otherwise. The writer of this Introduction likewise rejoices in the prodigious though admittedly disproportionate assemblage of paintings at the Prado. Yet the recent accessions are highly satisfying too, and given a few brief centuries of prosperity and security, the present magnificent though unbalanced collection might indeed become an equally magnificent balanced one.

PLATES

1. ANONYMOUS MASTER [*about 1475*] *The Archangel Michael* · Hispano-Flemish · 95¼ x 60¼"

2. BERMEJO [*active 1474-95*] *Santo Domingo de Silos* • Spanish

Painted 1474-77 • 95¼ x 51⅛″

19. EL GRECO [*1541-1614*] *The Resurrection* • Spanish
Painted about 1608 • 108 x 50″

20. EL GRECO [1541-1614] *St. John the Evangelist* • Spanish

Painted about 1596-1604 • 35⅜ x 30¼″

29. VELAZQUEZ [*1599-1660*] *The Dwarf Francisco Lezcano* • Spanish

Painted 1638-42 • 42⅛ x 32⅝"

30. VELAZQUEZ [*1599-1660*] *A Garden at the Villa Medici, Rome* · Spanish
Painted 1649-50 · 18⅞ x 16½″

35. ZURBARAN [1598-1664] *St. Luke Painting the Crucified Christ* • Spanish
Painted about 1660 • 41⅜ x 33⅛"

36. ZURBARAN [*1598-1664*] *Still Life* · Spanish · Painted about 1632-34 · 18⅛ x 33⅜"

37. VELAZQUEZ [1599-1660] *The Adoration of the Magi* · Spanish

Painted 1619 · 79⅞ x 49¼″

38. VELAZQUEZ [1599-1660] *The Venerable Mother Jerónima de la Fuente* · Spanish
Painted 1620 · 63 x 43¼″

45. VELAZQUEZ [1599-1660] *Queen Mariana of Austria*

(detail of plate 44)

46. VELAZQUEZ [1599-1660] *The Spinners (Las Hilanderas)* or *The Fable of Arachne* · Spanish · Painted about 1657 · 84⅝" x 113¾"

47. VELAZQUEZ [*1599-1660*] *The Spinners* (detail of plate 46)

48. VELAZQUEZ [1599-1660] *Philip IV Aged about Fifty* · Spanish

Painted about 1655 · 27⅛ x 22″

50. VELAZQUEZ [1599-1660] *A Garden at the Villa Medici, Rome* (detail of plate 30)

51. VELAZQUEZ [*1599-1660*] *Self-Portrait*

(detail of *The Maids of Honor*, plate 31)

52. CANO [*1601-67*] *The Virgin with the Effulgence* · Spanish

Painted about 1630-40 · 64⅛ x 42⅞"

53. CARRENO [*1614-85*] *Charles II* • Spanish

Painted 1673 • 79⅛ x 55½"

54. MURILLO [*1618-82*] *A Galician Girl with a Coin* · Spanish
Painted about 1645-50 · 24¾ x 16⅞″

55. MURILLO [1618-82] *Rebecca and Eliezer* · Spanish · Painted about 1650 · 42⅛ x 67⅞"

56. MURILLO [*1618-82*] *The Immaculate Conception* · Spanish

Painted about 1665-70 · 81⅛ x 56¾"

57. MURILLO *[1618-82] St. Anne Teaching the Virgin* · Spanish

Painted about 1660 · 86¼ x 65″

58. GOYA [*1746-1828*] *The Snowstorm* • Spanish

Painted 1786 • 108¼ x 115⅝"

59. GOYA [*1746-1828*] *Flower Girls* · Spanish

Painted 1786 · 109 x 75⅜″

60. GOYA [*1746-1828*] *Flower Girls*

(detail of plate 59)

61. GOYA [*1746-1828*] *Doña Tadea Arias de Enríquez* • Spanish
Painted 1790-95 • 74¾ x 41¾″

62. GOYA [*1746-1828*] *General José de Urrutia* • Spanish

Painted 1798 • 78¾ x 53⅛″

63. GOYA *[1746-1828] The Colossus* · Spanish

Painted about 1820 · 45⅝ x 41⅜"

68. GOYA [1746-1828] *The Family of Charles IV* (detail of plate 67)

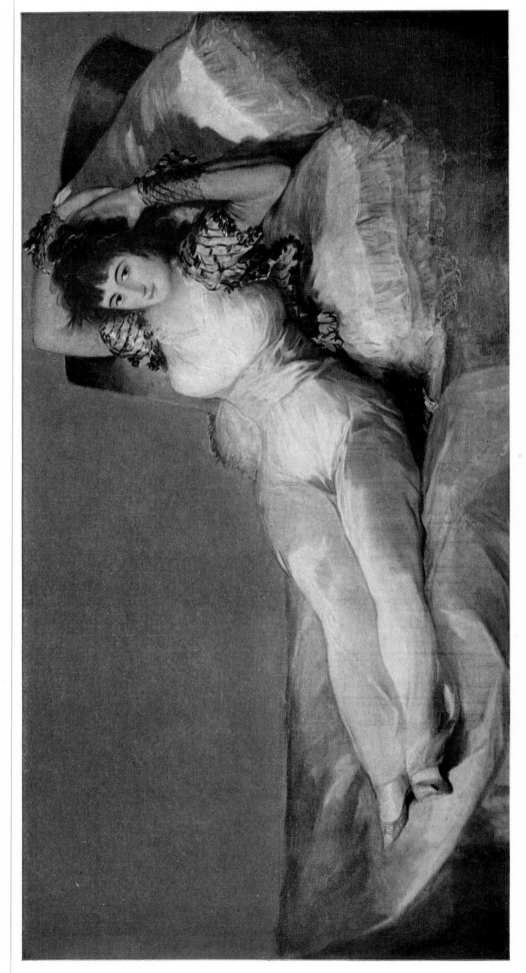

69. GOYA [1746-1828] *Maja Clothed* · Spanish · Painted about 1796-98 · 37⅞ x 74¾"

74. VAN EYCK SCHOOL [*Fifteenth Century*] *The Fountain of Living Water* • Flemish
Painted about 1450 • 71¼ x 45⅝″

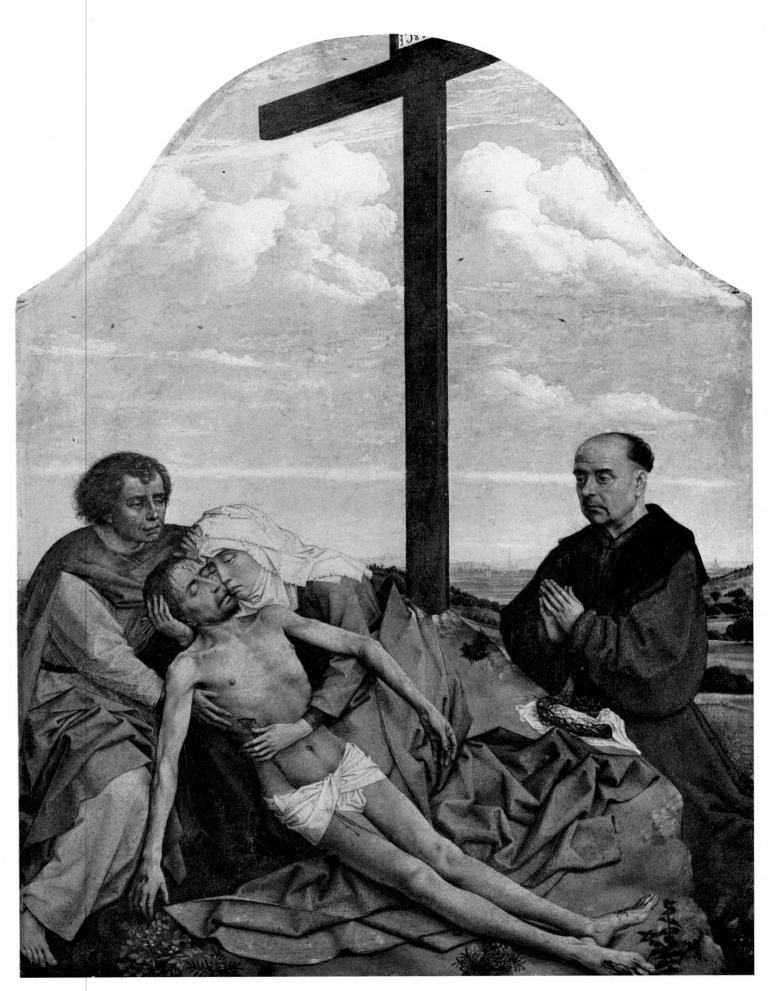

75. VAN DER WEYDEN [*1400-64*] *The Pietà* · Flemish

Painted 1440-50 · 18½ x 13¾″

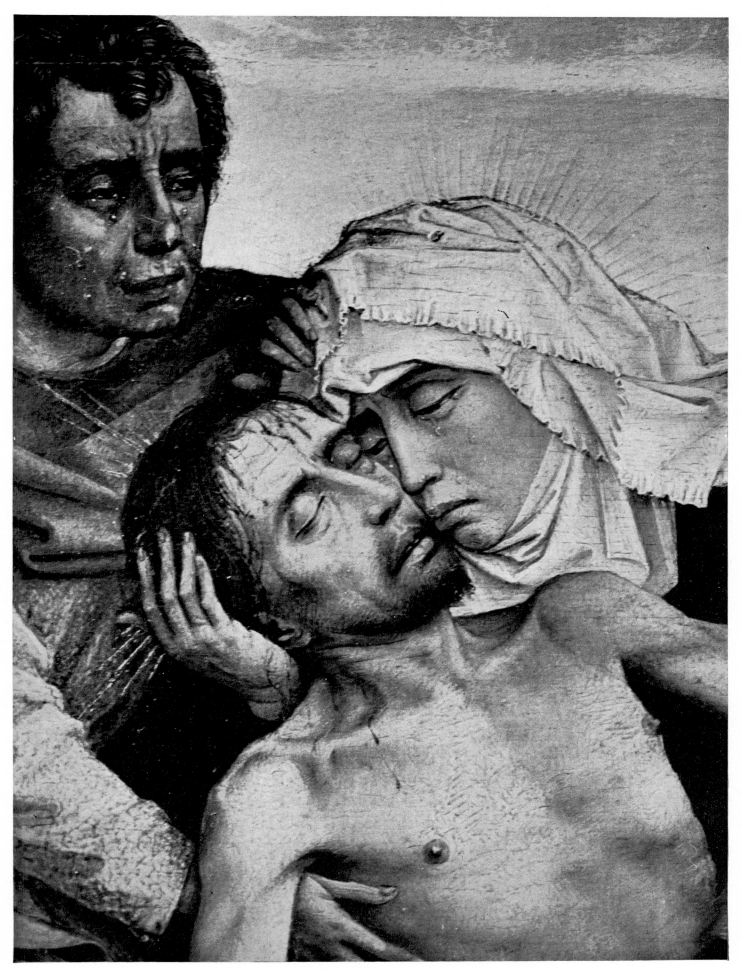

76. VAN DER WEYDEN [1400-64] *The Pietà*

(detail of plate 75)

77. Attributed to DIERIC BOUTS *[about 1420-75] The Visitation* • Flemish
Painted about 1450 • 31½ x 22"

78. Attributed to DIERIC BOUTS [*about 1420-75*] *The Adoration of the Magi* · Flemish
Painted about 1450 · 31½ x 20⅞″

79. Attributed to DIERIC BOUTS [*about 1420-75*] *The Visitation* (detail of plate 77)

80. MEMLING [*about 1433-94*] *The Adoration of the Magi* • Flemish • Painted about 1470 • 37⅞ x 57⅛"

81. MEMLING [*about 1433-94*] *The Nativity* • Flemish

Painted about 1470 • 37⅜ x 24¾"

82. MEMLING [*about 1433-94*] *The Nativity*

(detail of plate 81)

83. BOSCH [*about 1450-1516*] *A Child of Saturn* (exterior of *The Hay Wagon* triptych, closed) · Dutch

Painted about 1510 · 53⅛ x 35⅝″

84. BOSCH [*about 1450-1516*] *The Hay Wagon*

(detail of plate 114)

85. GERARD DAVID [*about 1450-1523*] *The Rest on the Flight into Egypt* • Flemish

Painted about 1510 • 23⅜ x 15⅝"

86. VAN ORLEY [*about 1492-1542*] *The Virgin of Louvain* · Flemish

Painted about 1516 · 17¾ x 15⅜"

87. PATINIR [*about 1480-1524*] *The River Styx* · Flemish · Painted about 1510 · 25¾ x 40½"

88. PATINIR [*about 1480-1524*] *The Rest on the Flight into Egypt* · Flemish · Painted about 1520 · 47⅜ x 69⅞"

89. GOSSAERT [*1478-about 1536*] *The Virgin and Child* • Flemish

Painted about 1527 • 24¾ x 19⅝"

90. CAMPIN [*Master of Flémalle; about 1380-1444*] *St. John the Baptist and Henricus Werl* and *St. Barbara* · *Flemish*

Painted 1438 · Each panel, 39¾ x 18½″

91. VAN DER WEYDEN [1400-64] *The Descent from the Cross* • Flemish. • Painted about 1435 • 86⅝ x 103⅜"

92. VAN DER WEYDEN [*1400-64*] *The Virgin and Child* · Flemish

Painted about 1437 · 39⅞ x 20½"

93. Attributed to DIERIC BOUTS [*1420-75*] *The Nativity* • Flemish

Painted about 1450 • 31½ x 20⅞″

98. BALDUNG [*about 1484/5-1555*] *Harmony* or *The Three Graces* • German

Painted about 1540 • 59½ x 24″

99. SCOREL [1495-1562] *Portrait of a Humanist* • Dutch

Painted 1524-30 • 26⅜ x 20½"

100. DÜRER [1471-1528] *Portrait of an Unknown Man* • German
Painted 1524 • 19⅝ x 14⅛″

101. MARINUS VAN REYMERSWAELE [*about 1495-1567*] *A Banker and His Wife* · Dutch · Painted 1539 · 32⅝ x 38⅛"

107. BOSCH [*about 1450-1516*] *The Garden of Delights* (detail of plate 106)

108. BOSCH [*about 1450-1516*] *The Garden of Delights* (detail of plate 106)

109. BOSCH [*about 1450-1516*] *The Garden of Delights* (detail of plate 106)

110. BOSCH [*about 1450-1516*] *The Garden of Delights* (detail of plate 106)

126. RUBENS [1577-1640] *St. George and the Dragon* • Flemish

Painted 1607-08 • 119⅝ x 100¾"

127. RUBENS [1577-1640] *The Triumph of the Church and the Eucharist* · Flemish · Painted 1625-28 · 33⅞ x 35⅝"

128. RUBENS [1577-1640] *Italian Peasants Dancing* · Flemish · Painted 1636-40 · 28¾ x 41¾"

129. RUBENS [*1577-1640*] *The Three Graces* • Flemish

Painted 1639-40 • 87 x 71¼″

130. JORDAENS [1593-1678] *The Artist's Family in a Garden* • Flemish
Painted about 1624 • 71¼ x 73⅝"

131. VAN DYCK [1599-1641] *The Brazen Serpent* · Flemish · Painted 1618-20 · 80¾ x 92½"

132. VAN DYCK [1599-1641] *Diana and Endymion Spied Upon by a Satyr* · Flemish · Painted about 1626 · 56¾ x 64⅛"

133. VAN DYCK [1599-1641] *Sir Endymion Porter and Van Dyck* · Flemish · Painted 1632-33 · 46⅛ x 56¾"

135. MANTEGNA [*1431-1506*] *The Dormition of the Virgin* · Italian

Painted about 1462 · 21¼ x 16½"

136. RAPHAEL [1483-1520] *Portrait of a Cardinal* · Italian

Painted about 1510 · 31⅛ x 24″

137. RAPHAEL [1483-1520] *The Madonna of the Fish* · Italian

Painted about 1513 · 84⅜ x 62¼″

138. TITIAN [*1477-1576*] *Bacchanal* · Italian

Painted about 1518 · 68⅞ x 76"

139. TITIAN [1477-1576] *The Worship of Venus* · Italian

Painted about 1518 · 67¾ x 68⅞″

140. TITIAN [1477-1576] *Charles V on Horseback at the Battle of Mühlberg* · Italian
Painted 1548 · 130¾ x 97⅞"

141. TITIAN [1477-1576] *Danaë and the Shower of Gold* · Italian · Painted 1552-54 · 50¾ x 70⅞"

142. TITIAN [1477-1576] *The Entombment* • Italian • Painted 1559 • 53⅜ x 68⅞"

143. Attributed to GIORGIONE [1478-1510] *The Virgin with St. Anthony and St. Roch* • Italian • Painted about 1510 • 36¼ x 52⅜"

144. RAPHAEL SCHOOL [*Sixteenth Century*] *The Holy Family* ("*La Perla*") • Italian
Painted about 1518 • 56¾ x 45¼"

145. ANDREA DEL SARTO [1486-1531] *Portrait of a Woman (The Artist's Wife?)* · Italian

Painted about 1520 · 28¾ x 22"

146. PARMIGIANINO [*1503-40*] *Portrait of the Count of San Secondo* · Italian
Painted 1533-35 · 52⅝ x 38⅝

147. VERONESE [1528?-88] *Venus and Adonis* · Italian

Painted about 1580 · 83½ x 75¼"

148. BAROCCI [1526-1612] *The Nativity* • Italian

Painted about 1605 • 52¾ x 41⅜"

149. ARTEMISIA GENTILESCHI [1597-1651] *A Peasant Girl with Pigeons* · Italian
Painted about 1630 · 23⅜ x 18½″

150. TIEPOLO [*1696-1770*] Fragment: *An Angel Bearing a Monstrance* • Italian

Painted 1769 • 72⅞ x 70⅛"

151. TITIAN [1477-1576] *St. Margaret* · Italian

Painted about 1565 · 95¼ x 71⅜"

152. TITIAN [*1477-1576*] *Religion Succored by Spain* · Italian
Painted 1534; reworked about 1572 · 66⅛ x 66⅛"

153. TITIAN [1477-1576] *The Fall of Man* · Italian
Painted about 1570 · 94½ x 73¼"

154. TINTORETTO [1518-94] *Judith About To Slay Holophernes* • Italian • Painted about 1550 • 22⅞ x 46⅞"

155. TINTORETTO [1518-94] *Joseph and Potiphar's Wife* • Italian • Painted about 1550 • 21¼ x 46⅝"

156. TINTORETTO [1518-94] *Joseph and Potiphar's Wife* (detail of plate 155)

157. TINTORETTO [1518-94] *Gentleman with a Gold Chain* · Italian
Painted about 1550 · 40½ x 29⅞"

158. VERONESE [1528?-88] *Moses Saved from the Nile* · Italian

Painted about 1575 · 19⅝ x 16⅞"

COMMENTARIES

1 ANONYMOUS HISPANO-FLEMISH MASTER (about 1475). *The Archangel Michael.* Tempera on canvas glued to wood, 95¼ x 60¼"

This impressive picture, about eight feet in height, is clearly influenced by such Northern artists as Van der Weyden and Memling, and yet the angels have a charm characteristic of the International Style which flourished about 1400–25 in several parts of Europe beyond the Pyrenees. The Archangel Michael, wearing a red mantle, is gracefully yet vigorously using his sword against the evil dragon which represents Satan. Above, angelic choirs give resounding accompaniment to the battle, while on either side of the Archangel the good angels thrust the evil ones down from heaven. In the polished boss of the Archangel's shield is reflected the donor of the painting kneeling between his guardian angel and a devil who tries to make off with his soul.

The painting was bought in 1924 from the Hospital of San Miguel (Michael) in Zafra, a picturesque town south of Mérida in southwest Spain.

2 BARTOLOMÉ BERMEJO (active 1474–95). Spanish. *Santo Domingo de Silos.* Painted 1474–77. Tempera on wood, 95¼ x 51⅛"

Though as convincing as if done from life, this portrait is in fact an imaginary one, for Santo Domingo de Silos died four centuries before it was painted. The dominating character of the subject accords well with what is known of this Benedictine abbot. Domingo (or Dominic) was born in Navarre early in the eleventh century and became the prior of San Millán de la Cogolla, a monastery in the kingdom in which he was born. Later he moved to Old Castile, where King Ferdinand I gave him the ruined early monastery in Silos, and there he ruled as abbot from 1047 to 1073, restoring this foundation "spiritually and materially." Today the Romanesque

sculptures in the lower cloister of the monastery are probably the finest of the period in Spain.

The panel is the central part of an altarpiece of which the two flanking panels have disappeared. The altarpiece, commissioned in 1474, was not painted for the church at Silos, but for one dedicated to this Saint at Daroca, not far from Saragossa. The severe frontality of the figure gives strength to the painting, to which the artist has added glory by much use of gold and polychromy on the richly carved throne. The noted authority on Spanish painting, Chandler R. Post, tells us that according to the contract for the altarpiece the Saint was to be represented in full pontifical robes embroidered in gold, and seated on a chair carved with the Seven Virtues. They are Faith, Hope, and Charity (the theological virtues) at the top, and Prudence, Fortitude, Temperance, and Justice (the four ancient cardinal virtues) at the sides.

Bartolomé Bermejo, the painter, was born in Cordova and was sometimes mentioned with the middle name of Cárdenas. But since both Cárdenas and Bermejo mean bright red, Dr. Post suggests that the artist may merely have been redheaded. In its clarity and meticulous workmanship Bermejo's work shows primarily the influence of Flemish painting, but the drawing is modified by Spanish austerity.

3 PEDRO BERRUGUETE (active by 1477, died by 1504). Spanish. *St. Dominic Burning Books.* Painted about 1480–90. Tempera on wood, 66½ x 30¾"

This panel showing the burning of books belonged to an altarpiece of which a figure of St. Dominic, as Inquisitor, was the center. The altarpiece was originally in Santo Tomás at Avila, and in the nineteenth century came to the Museo de la Trinidad in Madrid.

The great St. Dominic (1170–1221) of the noble Guzmán family in Old Castile, became a figure of great international importance. In 1207 he journeyed to Rome and

received from the Pope a mission to preach to the Albigenses in the south of France, near Albi, who were spreading a form of heresy. He went to the infected region and persuaded the offending sect to submit their books, and his also, to an ordeal by fire. The books of the Albigenses burned merrily, but the book of the true faith provided by St. Dominic leaped miraculously from the fire each time it was thrown in.

The painter Pedro Berruguete is one of the most famous of the Spanish artists of his time. There is documentary proof that a Spanish painter named Pedro was employed in the Duke of Urbino's palace at Urbino in 1477, when Joos van Gent was at work there, and there are specialists in the history of Spanish painting who believe with good reason that the Spanish Pedro mentioned in the document of 1477 was Berruguete. They also believe, with less reason perhaps, that he painted the famous frieze of prophets in the Ducal Library.

4 SCHOOL OF RODRIGO DE OSONA (active about 1476–84). Spanish. *The Madonna and Child with a Knight of Montesa.* Painted about 1480. Tempera on wood, 40⅛ x 37¾"

At the left of the Virgin's throne stands St. Benedict in his black habit reading from a book; at the right in his white habit is St. Bernard of Clairvaux with his abbot's crozier. At his feet kneels the small figure of a solemn suppliant, the donor presumably, who wears the cross and gown of a knight of the military order of Montesa. This order, founded early in the fourteenth century to succeed the Knights Templar, is said to have derived its name from the now ruined castle of Montesa near Játiba in the province of Valencia.

The quality of the painting is exceptionally high for a Spanish work of the period. All the figures are admirably conceived and executed, the holy Infant with his charming waywardness being especially close to fine North Italian work. The rendition of the church interior is elaborate, but satisfyingly right.

227

To Master Rodrigo de Osona, an artist of the Valencian School, has been attributed also an *Adoration of the Magi* in the Musée Bonnat at Bayonne.

5 FERNANDO YÁÑEZ DE LA ALMEDINA (active about 1505–36). Spanish. *St. Catherine.* Painted about 1520. Tempera on wood, 83½ x 44⅛″

This life-size St. Catherine of Alexandria is universally accepted as by Yáñez. She is graceful, gentle, and blond, and the general color effect of the picture is likewise blond. The admirable architectural setting is a striking feature, especially in its introduction of a wall of convenient height upon which St. Catherine has been able to lay her holy book, the palm branch indicating her martyrdom, and likewise her crown, for she was a princess. Sánchez Cantón calls this a work of superior beauty, and Chandler R. Post calls it probably the artist's best, "considered as an unexaggerated ideal of girlish beauty with a fineness of craft to match this loveliness," adding the supposition that it constituted the center of a retable, perhaps made for the church of Santa Catalina in Valencia.

Yáñez, judging from his name, must have been born in the town of Almedina in the province of Ciudad Real. He seems to have formed his style in Italy, for his paintings reveal his familiarity with the work of several different painters such as Leonardo, Raphael, Michelangelo, and their followers, active in Florence early in the sixteenth century. A "Ferrando Spagnuolo" is recorded as having received wages in 1505 for assisting Leonardo da Vinci in painting his never completed *Battle of Anghiari* in the Florentine Palazzo Vecchio. This Ferrando (or Fernando) may have been our painter, although in his early years he was associated professionally with another Spaniard, Fernando de los Llanos, to whom the document could refer. The two Fernandos worked in the Cathedral of Valencia and elsewhere in that city from 1506 to 1513, and Yáñez by himself later worked for several years in Cuenca.

6 LUIS DE MORALES (about 1509–86). Spanish. *The Presentation of the Christ Child in the Temple.* Painted 1560–67. Oil on wood, 57½ x 44⅞″

This is one of the most surprising compositions by Morales that has survived. The placing of the altar diagonally and off to one side of the picture is contrary to the universal practice of the Italian painters, who center it commandingly in their compositions. Still stranger are the damsels (called *doncellas* in the Prado catalogue). These *doncellas* with their offerings and their long, lighted candles move forward authoritatively and with an august rhythm, while the off-verticals of their tapers create tingling disharmonies with the strict verticality of the architecture.

The reader is probably familiar with the Biblical verses concerning the ancient Simeon in the second chapter of Luke, which the picture illustrates: "And it was revealed unto him by the Holy Ghost that he should not see death, before he had seen the Lord's Christ." When Mary and Joseph had brought the Child to him, he was ready at last to depart in peace (see also Memling's rendition of the subject, plate 94).

According to the Spanish scholar José Gudiol, the Prado's painting of the Presentation was a wing of a retable which was originally in the Treasure House, an annex to the Alcázar in Madrid. The Prado catalogue informs us simply that the panel was bought by Charles IV. Both data could be correct.

7 LUIS DE MORALES (about 1509–86). Spanish. *The Virgin and Child.* Painted about 1570. Oil on wood, 33⅛ x 25¼″

Because his paintings are characterized by probably the most intense mysticism of any Spanish-born painter, Morales has always been popularly known in Spain as *El Divino*. Like most artists who are largely self-taught, his compositions are surprising, even in instances where there is a known work from which he derived his idea. Thus, in a recent monograph on Morales, E. du Gué Trapier points to the Prado's *Holy Family* by Luini, which Morales could have known, and which contains the infants Jesus and John. Morales employs this well-known motive of the Leonardo school for a picture of his own, but where Luini's Virgin is an ample, normal woman, Morales' Queen of Heaven becomes extravagantly long-limbed, slender-throated, heavy-lidded, and utterly remote from mundane matters.

The Prado's *Virgin and Child* by Morales, which came in the bequest of Pablo Bosch, is one of several of this type, and probably the finest among them. An elegant, reduced replica less than twelve inches in height belongs to the National Gallery in London. In this subject Morales has remained closer to normal forms. Yet the aristocratic refinement of the lovely Virgin is in a class apart, and the parallel which has been drawn with Raphael seems farfetched. Indeed Morales' types, with their high and bony brows, seem closer to such Flemish painters as Hugo van der Goes and Joos van Gent.

Luis de Morales was born at Badajoz in Estremadura and spent his life—to the age of seventy-seven years, according to Palomino—working there and in neighboring towns. The same writer states that he studied, presumably in Seville, with Pedro de Compaña, a Fleming who had emigrated to Spain.

8 ALONSO SÁNCHEZ COELLO (about 1531/2–88). Spanish. *Two Daughters of Philip II.* About 1571. Oil on canvas, 53½ x 58⅝″

These prim little children are the daughters of Philip II and his third wife Isabelle de Valois. The older of the two girls, Infanta

Isabella Clara Eugenia, was born August 12, 1566, so that, for all her aplomb, her age when she posed for this painting must have been only five years! Her little sister, the Infanta Catalina Micaela, a year younger, was born October 10, 1567. Both little girls wear full court costumes, the skirts not as bouffant as they will be in later years but showing the trend, as the saying goes in *haut-couturier* circles. The high position of the little girls is signified by caps edged with pearls, that of the Infanta Isabella being significantly larger. The wreath of flowers and the flowers on the table are the only concessions granted to childhood.

In 1599 Philip II ceded the Spanish Netherlands to Isabella Clara as a marriage portion when she married the Archduke Albert. She died in Brussels in 1633 at the age of sixty-seven years. Her younger sister married Charles Emmanuel of Savoy in 1585, dying in Turin in 1597.

Sánchez Coello, the painter of this quaint double portrait, was born in the province of Valencia about 1531. He spent his youth in Lisbon, but later came to Madrid where Anthonis Mor was the chief influence on his style. Although Coello never equaled the Flemish master, he did succeed to his post as Court Painter when Mor fell into disfavor. In the Prado there are ten portraits by Coello. He died in Madrid, having carried on the tradition of formal, carefully detailed portraiture, which was maintained for twenty years more by Pantoja de la Cruz and other painters not positively identified.

9 JUSEPE DE RIBERA (1591–1652). Spanish. *The Magdalene in Prayer.* Painted about 1642–45. Oil on canvas, 71¼ x 76¾″

Ribera had the gift of seizing a moment of highest intensity in whatever story he was painting. This inspired sense of the exact moment is well shown in the painting which reveals Mary Magdalene in the exaltation of her penitence, kneeling at the mouth of her cave in the desert.

Her improvised *prie-dieu* consists here of several blocks of stone with her attribute, a pot of ointment, on the foremost stone. Her off-the-shoulder drapery, falling in rich, graceful folds, is almost impiously becoming, but her essential humility is shown in her bare feet and unbound hair. Her placement in a cave permits Ribera to exercise his magnificent command of light and shade for dramatizing the episode and for showing the beautiful face, hands, and feet of his subject.

The wistful and serious face of the saint conforms well with her legendary description —that of a woman of intelligence, capable of deep penitence and a genuine adoration of her Savior. The model for this painting was Ribera's own daughter, the unfortunate Margarita, who served as model again in the Dresden Gallery's beautiful *St. Agnes*. Margarita, who was born in 1630, was represented in a portrait drawing, which until World War II was in the Filangieri Museum, Naples. She became the mistress of Don Juan José of Austria, a bastard son of Philip IV.

Ribera, one of the greatest of the Spanish

painters, was born in Játiba, a small village in the hills south of Valencia, where his father Simon was a shoemaker. At an early age, twenty or thereabouts, Ribera went to Italy, soon reaching Naples which was then a possession of Spain. He remained in Naples for the rest of his life, dying there in 1652. It is said that although he lived most of his life in Italy, he never learned the language properly. Because of his persistent Spanishness, coupled presumably with a small stature, he was generally known in Italy as *Lo Spagnoletto*. He painted many important pictures for the successive art-loving viceroys from Spain, and some of his greatest for the Monastery of San Martino on the hill behind the city. His art may have been influenced by Ribalta, as the traditional account of him claims, but his early works, before his mid-thirties, are unidentified. In an article on the artist (*Art Bulletin*, March 1953) Delphine Fitz Darby says, "Ribera does not employ line to drive the eye but seeks to catch the one most telling moment in the course of movement. . . . Grave and rapt, [he moves] with a lofty rhythm, mingling rude strength and exquisite grace, now lapsing into monotonous repetition, now rising to an exalted pitch."

10 JUSEPE DE RIBERA (1591–1652). Spanish. *Jacob's Dream.* Painted 1639. Signed, lower right: *Jusepe de Ribera, español, F. 1639.* Oil on canvas, 70½ x 91¾"

The patriarch Jacob, here a youngish man, lies dreaming on a rocky ground immersed in a flood of golden light sent with his dream from a divine source. The scene is utterly quiet; the heavy figure drugged in sleep is no more idealized than any peasant resting at noontime. The Biblical source is in Genesis 28:10–12: "And Jacob went out from Beersheba, and went toward Haran. And he lighted upon a certain place, and tarried there all night, because the sun was set; and he took of the stones of that place, and put them for his pillows, and lay down in that place to sleep. And he dreamed, and behold, a ladder set up on the earth, and the top of it reached to heaven: and behold the angels of God ascending and descending on it."

The composition of the painting is unusually forceful. The figure, braced by the right hand pressed against the ground and the feet held far apart, forms a thrust which is compensated by the half-fallen tree.

11 FRAY JUAN BAUTISTO MAINO (1568–1649). Spanish. *The Reconquest of Bahía.* Painted about 1630–34. Oil on canvas, 121⅝ x 150"

Bahía de Todos los Santos ("Bay of all Saints"), a Brazilian port leading to the city of Salvador, was loosely claimed by the Spanish crown but was occupied by the Dutch West India Company in 1624. In the following year, Spain and Portugal joined in sending a fleet to recapture the port. This painting celebrating its reconquest was executed for the Hall of Kingdoms in the palace of Buen Retiro. Together with eleven other canvases commemorating victories of Philip IV's reign —including the famous *Surrender of Breda* by Velázquez (plate 27)—it was installed there in 1635.

The scene is laid above the bay with warships at anchor, a delightful *plein-air* rendition. Maino's blond color and pervasive light are exceptional. In a curious gathering of the most casual informality, triumphant soldiers lounge, intermingled with citizens of the town and people dressing the wounds of an unfortunate man. At the right the ceremonial purpose of the gathering is made clear. Don Fadrique de Toledo, Marqués de Villanueva, the leader of the expedition, addresses an audience of respectful military onlookers, as he points toward a tapestry depicting Philip IV crowned with a wreath by Victory and accompanied by his chief minister, the Count-Duke of Olivares. At the King's feet are the vanquished bodies of Heresy, Anger, and War.

Maino was a Dominican monk born near Milan in 1568. Having come to Spain, he became a drawing master of Philip IV. He was working in Toledo by 1611 and spent the rest of his life in Spain. It is hard to identify the origin of his style, though it is perhaps influenced by the deliberate casualness of Annibale Carracci and the older Bassani.

12 EL GRECO (1541–1614). Spanish. *The Baptism of Christ.* Painted about 1597–1600. Oil on canvas, 137¾ x 56¾"

This artist, whose real name was Domenicos Theotocopoulos, was popularly known in Spain as Dominico Greco, or simply "The Greek." He was born in Crete, then a Venetian possession. He must have begun to paint in the Byzantine icon tradition, which still evidences itself in some of the compositions of his maturity. At some time in his twenties El Greco went to Venice where he probably studied with Titian and was influenced by Jacopo Bassano and Tintoretto. In 1570 he went to Rome and came under the influence of Michelangelo's work. Before 1577, probably about 1575, El Greco moved to Spain, settling permanently in Toledo. The present Casa del Greco in that city is a small remaining portion of the palace of the Marqués de Villena, in which El Greco rented an apartment in 1585–86 and again during the last ten years of his life. For churches and convents in Toledo, he painted many works in his increasingly distorted and emotional style. He was successful, although little patronized by Philip II, who seems not to have been aware that El Greco's art was perfectly suited to the febrile mood of the Escorial.

This *Baptism* is one of several pictures that El Greco painted for the church of the Augustinian College in Madrid, founded by Doña Maria de Córdova y Aragón, a lady-in-waiting to Queen Anna, Philip II's fourth wife. The painter, who was responsible also for much of the architecture and sculpture in this church, received the commission for *The Baptism of Christ* late in 1596, from the Royal Council of Castile, with the stipulation that it was to be delivered on July 12, 1600. Since the Augustinian College was built on land donated by the King, and the order for the altarpiece given by a government body, the picture, in effect, was painted for Philip II, one of the three executed on royal order. The other two were *The Martyrdom of St. Maurice and the Theban Legion* and *The Dream of Philip II*, both in the Escorial.

Philip died before *The Baptism* was finished, and Greco had to bring suit to collect the money due him. The painting, though a typical work, is much calmer than the artist's very late treatment of the same subject in the Hospital of San Juan Bautista (Afuera). Five angels assist at the ceremony, holding up Christ's red robe behind him. A benign and quiet figure of God the Father looks on from above and the Holy Spirit descends as a dove amidst the tumultuous flapping of the wings of angels and cherubim. Attached to the rock on which Christ kneels is a paper bearing Greco's signature in Greek.

13 EL GRECO (1541–1614). Spanish. *The Baptism of Christ* (detail of plate 12)

The pictorial style in which El Greco clothes his mystical fervor relies to a large extent on forced contrasts of light and dark like those of the *tenebrosi* (followers of Caravaggio) whom he preceded by a full generation. In this detail showing the head, torso, and arms of the Baptist, without resorting to the heavy shadows which the *tenebrosi* were to use, he models powerfully, almost violently, pushing into light the ribs, collar bone, cheekbone, ear, and eyelid.

14 EL GRECO (1541–1614). Spanish. *St. Andrew and St. Francis.* Painted about 1603. Oil on canvas, 65¾ x 44½"

This painting, which F. J. Sánchez Cantón in the Prado catalogue rightly describes as a superlatively beautiful picture in a remarkably fine state of preservation, came to light during the Spanish civil war of 1936–39. Its very existence was entirely unknown in art-historical circles until it was brought to the Prado for safekeeping from the Community of the Royal Monastery of the Incarnation in Madrid. The Prado acquired it in 1942.

St. Andrew, holding the great X-shaped cross which is the symbol of his martyrdom, with his white hair and scraggly beard, offers a strong contrast in type to the hooded figure of St. Francis, whose gesturing hands declare the completeness of his self-abnegation. Dark against the high light of the hand laid on St. Francis' breast Greco has painted the mark of the stigmata, witness to the Saint's mystical participation in Christ's Passion. The two Saints appear to be engaged in a purely theological, otherworldly discussion, the low horizon line and the suggestion of landscape in the fresh blue sky and bright clouds signifying that they have met together in some remote high place.

229

The figures of both these Saints were treated by El Greco in other pictures. In a private collection there is a painting of St. Andrew alone in a landscape, similar in gesture and pose, and the Prado owns a small painting of St. John the Evangelist with St. Francis, in which St. Francis appears with these same gestures and general appearance repeated.

15 EL GRECO (1541–1614). Spanish. *Portrait of Jerónimo de Cevallos*. Painted about 1610–12. Oil on canvas, 25¼ x 21¼″

The subject of this portrait has been identified from an engraving by Pedro Angel as the jurist and prefect (*regidor*) of Toledo, Jerónimo de Cevallos. Born in Escalona between 1559 and 1562, Cevallos was a writer of some importance, the author of several books on law and government written in Latin and in the vernacular Spanish.

Judging from the wide ruff, this portrait appears to be as late as 1610–12. The paint, as is typical of El Greco's work in his last years, is loaded heavily on the canvas, especially on the ruff, but also on the beard and flesh. In 1794 the painting was in the villa of the Duque del Arco, the source from which came most of the Prado's incomparable group of portraits by El Greco.

16 EL GRECO (1541–1614). Spanish. *The Pentecost* (detail of plate 22)

This detail from El Greco's painting of *The Pentecost* shows at the left the ecstatic, up-turned head of the Virgin Mary, and close beside, more absorbed in tender solicitude for the mother of her Lord than in her own experience, is Mary Magdalene, seen in sharp profile, her head swathed in the soft woolen drapery that sometimes appears in other paintings of women by El Greco. The third figure to the right of the Virgin, pictured in the guise of an apostle, appears to be a portrait, done from memory, of Don Antonio Covarrubias (1514–1601). Don Antonio was a great humanist and theologian, a canon of the Cathedral of Toledo, and also a jurisconsult and archaeologist. He sat in the epoch-making Council of Trent which initiated the Counter Reformation. In the Casa del Greco at Toledo are portraits by El Greco or by an assistant of Don Antonio and also of his brother the prelate, Diego de Covarrubias (1512–77), who was Bishop of Segovia and President of the Council of Castile.

17 EL GRECO (1541–1614). Spanish. *The Holy Trinity*. Completed by 1577. Oil on canvas 118⅛ x 70½″

This painting was the "attic" or top member of the high altar of Santo Domingo el Antiguo in Toledo, which El Greco finished in

1577, and is therefore one of the first works done by him after settling in Toledo.

Even if the date were not known, the smooth, solidly modeled flesh and the heroic proportions of the body of Christ, which recall Italian paintings of the late Renaissance, would plainly declare it an early work, in which the painter was still influenced by the art that he had looked at before coming to Spain. In the original ensemble the *Trinity* stood above *The Assumption of the Virgin* (now in the Art Institute of Chicago), which is about thirteen feet high. Since the *Trinity* is nearly ten feet in height, the whole altarpiece must have been enormous, as indeed most of the major altarpieces in Spain are. The lower part of the *Trinity*, which is filled by the billowing pedestal of cloud supporting the figures, was originally overlapped by an oval *Veronica's Veil*.

This kind of representation of the Holy Trinity, in which the body of the dead Christ is supported by God the Father, is known also as the Throne of Grace. The theme has a long tradition in the history of art, going back at least to the beginning of the fourteenth century, but it became an especial favorite of the Counter-Reformation; the sorrow of the Father for the suffering that He himself had ordained for the Son induced the intense contrition so characteristic of the religious emotions of the late sixteenth century. El Greco's composition is derived from Dürer's woodcut of the same subject made in 1511. But whereas Dürer's angels carry the instruments of the Passion, El Greco's simply hover about the majestic figure of the Almighty, underlining the divine grief with their own expression of mourning.

18 EL GRECO (1541–1614). Spanish. *Portrait of a Man with Hand on Breast*. Painted about 1577–80. Oil on canvas, 31⅞ x 26″

El Greco signed this portrait, as was his custom, in Greek, but used all capital letters, a form that he employed only in early works. The picture must therefore be dated at the beginning of his Spanish career, though the lace collar is not unlike some of the collars worn by the knights attending the burial of the Count of Orgaz in the famous painting in the Church of Santo Tomé, Toledo, contracted for in 1586.

The spirit of the painting, too, is like that of El Greco's most Spanish works, with the beautiful hand laid on the breast in solemn promise or attestation, and an expression combining graciousness and melancholy in the eyes and mouth of the elegant face. The sword hilt is of sculptured gold, and a medal or the badge of a military order hangs from a fine chain about the neck of the subject. Two Spanish scholars have identified him as Juan de Silva, Marqués de Montemayor, who was a Knight of Santiago and the chief notary of Toledo.

19 EL GRECO (1541–1614). Spanish. *The Resurrection*. Painted about 1608. Oil on canvas, 108 x 50″

Like *The Pentecost* (plate 22), this is a late picture, of the same size and with the same rounded top. The head of Christ, framed in a square nimbus, wears an expression of radiant tranquillity and detachment, proclaiming that not only death, but human life too, with its anxieties and suffering, have no more dominion over Him. He holds the banner of the Resurrection, and His brightly glowing, transfigured body seems to float upward, weightless and free. Only one of the soldiers who had been set to guard Him remains asleep and unware. The others fall backward in shock and dismay, or writhe in amazement. El Greco has introduced an original motive in the soldiers who have recovered themselves sufficiently to try violently with brandished swords to stop Christ's rising.

20 EL GRECO (1541–1614). Spanish. *St. John the Evangelist*. Painted about 1596–1604. Oil on canvas, 35⅜ x 30¼″

St. Isidore relates that an attempt was made in Rome to do away with St. John by poisoning the cup containing the Sacrament. St. John nevertheless drank and administered the Communion with no harm to himself or the others, because the poison issued miraculously from the chalice in the form of a serpent. The would-be assassin himself fell dead.

It is very probable that this three-quarterlength figure of the Beloved Disciple belonged originally to an *apostolado*. An *apostolado* was a series of separate panels representing the disciples, including sometimes a figure of Christ blessing and one of the Virgin of Sorrows.

Several such series by or attributed to El Greco are known. A set in the sacristy of the Cathedral of Toledo is complete except for St. John the Evangelist, and it is tempting to assume that the picture in the Prado is the missing one, were it not for the fact that the others are higher by more than three inches. The painting may well have been cut at the top, but it was probably not cut at the bottom, for the composition there closely resembles that in other pictures of St. John by the artist, and in its closely restricted composition is typical of El Greco's style.

21 EL GRECO (1541–1614). Spanish. *The Holy Family*. Painted 1594–1604. Oil on canvas, 42⅛ x 27⅛″

This painting, which is not signed, follows with some variations *The Holy Family* now in the Museo de San Vicente at Toledo, which came from the Hospitalillo de Santa Ana. The Toledo picture, which does bear El Greco's signature, is larger and more severe than the Prado version, and lacks the figure of St. Joseph, which however appears to have been included originally at the right and painted out. The Prado *Holy Family* comes from one of the convents which the State suppressed in 1835–36. It was apparently painted somewhat later than the version in Toledo.

230

22 EL GRECO (1541–1614). Spanish. *The Pentecost*. Painted about 1608. Oil on canvas, 108¼ x 50"

Few subjects are better adapted to the expression of El Greco's genius than this one, which was a spiritual experience of such overpowering intensity that it took concrete form perceptible to the sight and hearing of all those participating. The painting represents the promised descent of the Holy Spirit upon the disciples and intimates of Jesus on the Jewish feast of the Pentecost, fifty days after the Passover in which He was crucified.

The event is described with stark simplicity in the Acts of the Apostles 2:1–4: "And when the day of Pentecost was fully come, they were all with one accord in one place. And suddenly there came a sound from heaven as of a rushing mighty wind, and it filled all the house where they were sitting. And there appeared unto them cloven tongues like as of fire, and it sat upon each of them. And they were all filled with the Holy Ghost, and began to speak with other tongues, as the Spirit gave them utterance." The festival commemorating this event—called in English Whitsunday—is, after Easter and Christmas, the most important of the greats feasts of the Church and is celebrated on the seventh Sunday after Easter.

El Greco has composed his picture marvelously on ascending levels that lead the eye upward to the Virgin, and above her head to the Dove of the Holy Spirit. He has arranged the heads of the uppermost figures in an undulating horizontal line that clearly separates the events of earth from the manifestations of heaven. *The Pentecost* has the same dimensions and the same arched top as *The Resurrection* (plate 19), and like it was probably painted for an altarpiece made in the last decade of the painter's life, about 1608.

23 JUSEPE DE RIBERA (1591–1652). Spanish. *The Martyrdom of St. Bartholomew*. Signed on a rock, lower right: *Jusepe de Ribera español 1639* (or *1630*, last number illegible). Oil on canvas, 92⅛ x 92⅛"

In this painting Ribera shows St. Bartholomew being made ready for crucifixon by three ruffians, who have already bound his wrists cruelly to the lowered transverse bar of the cross and are now hoisting the body into place by means of ropes. The wide Y of the Saint's arms and torso, and the passionate protest of the legs, are tremendously dramatic yet without any recourse to hysterics. The same may be said of the townsfolk who watch the scene with quiet self-control. The eyes of the spectator are carried toward the top of the picture and beyond by the angles of the ropes.

In favor of the date 1639 rather than 1630 for this picture are the lucid shadows which show how far Ribera has left behind his earlier, more violent chiaroscuro. The composition has become grand and free, with all the forms easily legible. Although Ribera had been living in Naples for about thirty years, the heads of the onlookers at the lower left remain surprisingly non-Italian; in fact, they are utterly Spanish, resembling Goya's crowds except in texture.

There is some doubt, according to Delphine Fitz Darby, as to whether this painting actually represents St. Bartholomew, for Ribera's known representations of that Saint show him with a full gray beard. According to her argument, the subject is rather the crucifixion of another and younger apostle, Saint Philip, who is usually represented as beardless, and who was bound by ropes to the cross of his martyrdom.

24 FRANCISCO ZURBARÁN (1598–1664). Spanish. *St. Peter Nolasco's Vision of St. Peter the Apostle*. Signed lower center: *FRANCISCUS DE ZURBARAN/Faciebat* 1629. Oil on canvas, 70½ x 87¾"

St. Peter Nolasco was canonized in 1628. A year later, Zurbarán was commissioned to paint twenty-two episodes from the life of the Saint for the monastery of the Order of Our Lady of Mercy (the Mercedarians) in Seville, although he himself may not have painted the entire series. This canvas and plate 33 are among the four which are known today.

Peter Nolasco was born of a noble family in southern France somewhat before the year 1200. Disturbed by the heretical sects, he was impelled by his religious enthusiasm to leave France and go to Spain. There, after having exhausted his patrimony in ransoming Christian captives from the Moors, he founded the chivalrous military order of the *Merced Calzada* or Shod Mercedarians, approved in 1230 by Pope Gregory IX. Its members were laymen who devoted their fortunes and, if necessary, their freedom to redeeming Christian captives who had been enslaved by the Moors.

In this painting by Zurbarán, Nolasco suddenly experiences a vision of St. Peter, his patron saint, who having been condemned to death chose to be crucified head downward as a sign of humility. Zurbarán has made the vision of the elderly, inverted saint such a real presence that the beholder is almost jolted by the impact.

Zurbarán was born in the small town of Fuente de Cantos (Badajoz). He served his apprenticeship in Seville, but how his style developed is a mystery, for though his master's name is known, his works are not. It is enough that Zurbarán's bold, pictorial conceptions and his powerful modeling made it possible for him to paint some of the handsomest and most emotional pictures of religious persons and events in the history of Spanish painting. It was in consideration of his important undertaking for the Mercedarians in 1629 in Seville that young Zurbarán was officially invited by that city to take up his residence there.

25 DIEGO VELÁZQUEZ (1599–1660). Spanish. *The Topers* or *The Triumph of Bacchus*. Painted 1628–29. Oil on canvas, 65 x 88⅝"

Just before Velázquez started on his first visit to Italy in the summer of 1629, he received payment for this "painting of Bacchus, which he made in his Majesty's service." For all its liveliness, it is painted with a heavy brush and with strong shadows, and thus is still reminiscent of the *bodegones*—that Spanish (and especially Sevillian) form of extraordinarily naturalistic genre painting—which Velázquez had painted in Seville and in his first years after reaching Madrid. Unfortunately the Prado possesses none of the real *bodegones* by Velázquez, for the French generals made off with them in 1812.

Formerly known simply as *Los Borrachos* (*The Drunks* or *The Drinkers*) this painting is now recognized from the written record as a festival of the bibulous god of the ancients. But except for Bacchus himself, the characters taking part are regular Spanish types, even to the interloping beggar.

Was Velázquez representing an actual seventeenth-century grape harvest festival? The most enlightening answer is given by Ortega y Gasset when he writes, "Velázquez seeks for the root of each myth in what we might call the logarithm of reality. This he paints. There is no question then of ridicule or parody . . . he does not let himself be carried away into an imaginary world, but rather prevails upon it to come back to the world of reality."

The Triumph of Bacchus was originally wider (how much?), but was injured in one of the palace fires and cut down as a result.

26 DIEGO VELÁZQUEZ (1599–1660). Spanish. *Apollo at the Forge of Vulcan*. Painted 1630. Oil on canvas, 87¾ x 114½"

Here Apollo, crowned with laurel and haloed with a golden light, visits Vulcan working at his forge to inform him of the adultery of his wife Venus with Mars. Vulcan, the god of fire and the blacksmith of Olympus, is busy with his four assisting Cyclops forging armor for the gods. The picture was painted during Velázquez' visit to Rome in 1630, and the Spanish faces and haircuts of the Cyclops have led the art critic Carl Justi to suppose that members of the Spanish Ambassador's household in Rome served as models for them. Moreover, their bodies are said to reveal something of the bullfighter's nervous and elastic build.

The scene, as the artist has imagined it, is the breathless moment before surprise and comprehension are transformed into jealousy and vengeful action. The incident is localized and actualized, or modernized, in the same spirit as in *The Triumph of Bacchus* (plate 25), which was painted shortly before Velázquez left for Italy. As to the appropriateness of the Cyclops' facial expressions, however, it would not be easy to say where among Italian paintings Velázquez could have found anything so perfect.

27 DIEGO VELÁZQUEZ (1599–1660). Spanish. *The Surrender of Breda*. Finished by April 1635. Oil on canvas, 120⅞ x 144½"

This painting was one of twelve ordered by King Philip IV from various artists available to him at the time. All represented military triumphs which had been won during his reign, and all were hanging in the Hall of Kingdoms in the Palace of Buen Retiro when it was formally opened on April 28, 1635.

The representation of *The Surrender of Breda,* apportioned to Velázquez, celebrated one of Spain's greatest victories, for it terminated the eight-months' siege of an almost impregnably fortified city. The scene depicted by Velázquez had occurred on June 5, 1625. The Dutch commander, Justin of Nassau, was chivalrously permitted to march his men out of Breda in good order and was personally and graciously received by Marchese Ambrogio Spínola, the Genoese soldier of fortune who commanded the Spanish army.

Usually called "The Lances" (*Las Lanzas*) in Spain, this is one of Velázquez' most famous compositions. Critics have pointed out several paintings and engravings showing lances against the sky as possible sources of this picturesque device, but none develops it to a degree comparable to this work by Velázquez with its twenty-five positive verticals. In this picture the artist as always searches out the human aspects of the event. It was one which he had to imagine, for he had not witnessed it. He has individualized each face, and has supposed that the long and exhausting siege must have left the troops with little interest in such a formality as the surrender of a key.

Velázquez knew Spínola's appearance, for on his first trip to Italy in 1629 he sailed from Barcelona to Genoa on the same ship with him. His version of the Marchese's face is far less harsh than that which Rubens painted in 1625. A curious and unexplained relation exists between the *The Surrender of Breda* and Rubens' painting made in the same year, which shows the two Ferdinands shaking hands in the presence of their troops, before the battle of Nördlingen.

28 DIEGO VELÁZQUEZ (1599–1660). Spanish. *Prince Baltasar Carlos on His Pony.* Painted about 1634. Oil on canvas, 82¼ x 68⅛"

The portrait of this engaging princeling is one of many likenesses of him, others being in the Museum of Fine Arts, Boston, and the Wallace Collection, London. Today it would surely be said that the child is highly photogenic, what with his erect carriage, his alert eyes, and his little mouth firmly closed, and with it all his air of imperious control. His age could be four and a half to five years. His black tunic contrasts with sleeves of gold cloth, and he wears the official pink sash correctly placed and streaming in the breeze, together with an imposing, slightly tilted plumed hat snugly fitted to his head but showing the childish fair hair at one side. His baton, held commandingly in his right hand, signifies the power of his position. The pony is curveting, and the day is glorious for a ride. Even the bushes and trees seem to swirl backward in opposition to the pony's frisky leaps.

Prince Baltasar Carlos was born October 17, 1629, the son of Philip IV by his first wife, Isabella of France. He died in Saragossa in

October 1646 at the age of seventeen years, destined never to ascend the throne which he was to have inherited.

This portrait of him riding his pony was painted as an overdoor in the Hall of Kingdoms at Buen Retiro. Doubtless it was because the picture was to hang high that Velázquez showed the pony's barrel from underneath.

29 DIEGO VELÁZQUEZ (1599–1660). Spanish. *The Dwarf Francisco Lezcano.* Painted 1638–42. Oil on canvas, 42⅛ x 32⅝"

In the earlier centuries when travel was difficult, entertainment in the palaces was found in various forms. Among the courts of Europe it was customary to maintain distorted human creatures, dwarfs—sometimes clever, sometimes mental defectives, and more often than not repulsive in appearance. Among them were buffoons, vestiges of the medieval clown in cap and bells who was privileged to twit his master with sharp remarks and bold jests. These were the clever ones. Many a portrait exists of a noble personage painted with a favorite dwarf, for some of the dwarfs were decidedly companionable. Later came the craze also for tiny colored children whose portraits were painted accompanying their amused mistresses.

Velázquez painted these warped and stunted courtiers with complete respect, showing them as they were, seeing them with as much clarity and freedom from prejudice as he saw their masters. The dwarf in the present portrait—Francisco Lezcano by name —was from Vizcaya, a Basque province, and belonged to young Baltasar Carlos. He is shown sitting out-of-doors against a rock and holding a playing card.

This superb portrait, like a modern clinical record, reveals with unsurpassed subtlety the appearance of a typical cretin. The enlarged head, the slack posture with the puffy, folded hands, the loose out-turned feet, all betray the poor creature's abnormality. The placid vacancy of his face appears to express good nature and an inane complacency, perhaps simply his pride at having his picture painted like his fellow dwarfs. Although plainly a *loco,* not a buffoon, this dwarf was for a time expelled from the court because his remarks and jests were too coarse and vile to stomach.

30 DIEGO VELÁZQUEZ (1599–1660). Spanish. *A Garden at the Villa Medici, Rome.* Painted 1649–50. Oil on canvas, 18⅞ x 16½"

Velázquez' view at the Villa Medici, in the subdued light of late afternoon, was formerly supposed to have been painted during the artist's first visit to Italy in 1630, for it was then that he was lodged for several weeks in the villa. However, critics are now agreed that the thin painting, the tender brushwork, and the deeper understanding of textures and light reveal the qualities of the Velázquez of twenty years later.

The Villa Medici, on the Pincian Hill near the church of the Santissima Trinità de' Monti, contains gardens with dignified architectural features and classical statues. In this late afternoon view Velázquez chose a wall with a marble balustrade above, and a noble Palladian entrance leading to dark cypresses beyond. But all this civilized splendor and beauty is offset by the ramshackle boards of the repair crew and by the maid hanging a cloth to dry from the balustrade. Such calculatedly informal pictorial elements are surprisingly advanced for the mid-seventeenth century—indeed not usual before the work of Hubert Robert and Fragonard in the last part of the eighteenth. To see again such subtle and truthful observation of subdued light and marvelously rendered textures one must wait for Corot's views of the Eternal City. Velázquez painted a companion picture (also in the Prado) using another part of the villa and showing it in the sparkling sunshine of midday.

31 DIEGO VELÁZQUEZ (1599–1660). Spanish. *The Maids of Honor (Las Meninas).* Painted 1656. Oil on canvas, 125¼ x 108⅝"

So famous is Velázquez' greatest painting, *The Maids of Honor,* that it is known generally as *Las Meninas* even by travelers unfamiliar with Spanish. (In fact, the word is originally Portuguese, meaning simply "maidens.") In Madrid, the painting is given a gallery of its own, just as Raphael's *Sistine Madonna* used to have its room in Dresden, and Giorgione's *Tempest* did in Venice.

This masterpiece by Velázquez is arranged with touching naturalness and easy informality. Eleanora Duse is reported to have exclaimed that it was great "royal theater." The entire scene was painted from an image in an unseen mirror which must have been placed about where we, the spectators, would stand. The artist is seen quietly at work on his canvas which appears to have about the same height as the actual painting. The room is a large one in the old Alcázar, and the windows at the right have all been shuttered excepting one or two up forward. From there comes most of the light, distributing itself not with the usual baroque violence but with a more polite, more vaporous vivacity, with an incomparably satisfying expression of tender enveloping air.

The prima donna of the occasion is Doña Margarita of Austria, the five-year-old daughter of Philip IV and his second Queen, Mariana. At one side of the little princess one of the *meninas* kneels affectionately, offering a drink of water. She is Doña María Augustina Sarmiento. At her other side stands Isabel de Velasco. Both Maids of Honor were daughters of noble houses passing a year or two at court before entering into marriage. The little Princess remains sweet but inattentive. In the foreground the old mastiff would like to sleep, but the tiny dwarf Nicolasito prods him. The clumsy buffoon Maribárbola watches herself in the big mirror. At the back of the room in a small mirror are seen reflected the King and Queen, while beside this mirror a startling rectangle of light strikes in as the palace superintendent opens a door. In *Las Meninas,* as Sánchez Cantón has remarked, stiff ceremonial is replaced by everyday life. "Protocol gives way to the heart of man," and one learns more from the picture than from volumes analyzing the Spanish character.

32 DIEGO VELÁZQUEZ (1599–1660). Spanish. *The Spinners,* or *The Fable of Arachne* (detail of plate 46)

The actual subject of this major and technically culminating work by Velázquez, popularly called *The Spinners,* has been known for only a few years (see commentary for plate 46). The girls shown in this detail are working in the lower room of a tapestry factory where the dim, uneven light is undeniably beautiful and moreover probably satisfied the workers, for to this day in Spain women are everywhere to be seen deliberately choosing shadowy corners in which to work at their lace or embroidery.

The principal figure in this detail, with her sensitive left hand guiding the yarn for winding, has been compared with sibyls and fates as painted by the Italian masters. But, with his characteristic love of the everyday life around him, Velázquez had made his spinner's youth and gentleness evident although her face is turned away. Michelangelo would at least have approved of the placing of her left foot which gives such perfect stability to the figure, balancing as it does the force of the busy, extended arm.

33 FRANCISCO ZURBARÁN (1598–1664). Spanish. *St. Peter Nolasco's Vision of the New Jerusalem.* Painted 1629–30. Signed near the hem of an angel's tunic: *Fᶜᵒ Dez.F.* Oil on canvas, 70½ x 87¾"

This is another of the four known surviving episodes of the life of St. Peter Nolasco from the series which Zurbarán painted for the monastery of the Mercedarians in Seville (see plate 24). Here the Saint, dressed in the white habit of his Order, has fallen asleep while kneeling to meditate on a holy book. In a dream an angel in pale blue and pink appears to him and points to the Promised Land, the New Jerusalem (looking in Zurbarán's picture much like the towered walls of Avila with people coming and going through the gates).

It is the same ecstatic vision that John the Evangelist described in Revelation 21:2: "And I, John, saw the holy city, the new Jerusalem, coming down from God out of heaven, prepared as a bride adorned for her husband." And again in Revelation 21:9–10: "And there came unto me one of seven angels . . . and shewed me that great city, the holy Jerusalem, descending out of heaven from God."

34 FRANCISCO ZURBARÁN (1598–1664). Spanish. *St. Casilda.* Painted 1638–42. Oil on canvas, 72½ x 37¾"

When Zurbarán painted the monks in the religious houses of Spain as he so often did, and when he represented the tense dramas of saintly lives, he dealt with what was for him the most real, the most vibrantly tangible, of all experienced things. Probably the closest he ever came to fantasy or frivolity was in his figures of lady-saints. These, besides wearing sumptuous and improbable costumes made in the richest of colors and cut from the heaviest of brocades, are liberally provided with jewels. Moreover they have distinctly individual faces and are apt to gaze directly, even boldly, at the spectator.

According to the most credible theory, they are not saints at all, but pretty Sevillian ladies each provided with the price of a portrait and with a vivid desire to be shown on canvas in the guise of her patron saint—only, *por favor,* more becomingly dressed! Although Zurbarán (and his assistants) made many of these enchanting and admirable pot-boilers, he did occasionally paint a female saint seriously, when the expression of modesty and virtue is unmistakable and very, very different from the ladies under discussion.

In the Prado's portrait of Señorita Casilda, whoever she may have been, she is dressed most elegantly and displays her patron saint's attribute of flowers held in her upraised outer skirt. The real St. Casilda was the daughter of a Moorish emir of Toledo in the eleventh century. Like the better known St. Elizabeth of Thuringia, she disobeyed a parental regulation in charitably carrying bread in her skirt to the hungry. When her disobedience was on the point of discovery the bread miraculously turned into roses.

The Prado's *Casilda* has evidently lost four to five inches of canvas at the left. If these saints were indeed painted in series, she may have belonged with the saucy, barefoot shepherdess *St. Margaret* in London and the demure *St. Rufina* at the Hispanic Society in New York.

35 FRANCISCO ZURBARÁN (1598–1664). Spanish. *St. Luke Painting the Crucified Christ.* Painted about 1660. Oil on canvas, 41⅜ x 33⅛"

The legend of St. Luke gives him credit for painting portraits of Christ as well as of the Virgin. Hence the intensely devout painter represented in this canvas, for want of clearer indications, may be called St. Luke. Yet his face with its low forehead, its salient nose, and its scraggy beard is not the conventional conception of an evangelist. On the contrary it is unquestionably a portrait. But whose? One would like to call it Zurbarán's self-portrait, but there is no acceptable likeness of Zurbarán for comparison. The red-chalk drawing in the Louvre labeled as such is unconvincing, and the engraving published by Stirling-Maxwell in volume III of his *Annals of the Artists of Spain* is a dandified and romanticized absurdity. Thus, who can disprove that this is a likeness of the powerfully emotional painter that we know, the somewhat seedy looking country-bred fellow whose life we have read about?

36 FRANCISCO ZURBARÁN (1598–1664). Spanish. *Still Life.* Painted about 1632–34. Oil on canvas, 18⅛ x 33⅛"

Arranged in a row on a brown table, against a dark background are, from left to right: a gilded cup resting in a shallow pewter dish; an amphora of white pottery; a second amphora with a narrow neck in red pottery; and finally, resting in a second pewter dish, a wine pot, or *cantarilla,* fluted and covered with a white glaze. Although this still life is not signed, similar objects in metal and pottery are to be found in some of Zurbarán's signed religious paintings, and it seems clear that they were studio properties.

The painting is a stimulating essay in the textures of inanimate objects, and it serves to indicate and isolate this field of Zurbarán's versatility. Another version of this still life is in the Barcelona Museum, and a signed and dated (1633) painting with a basket of oranges as its center is in the collection of Count Contini-Bonacossi in Florence. It has the same shallow pewter dishes as in our still life. This work, similar to the Prado's in spirit, was praised by the authority on Spanish painting, August L. Mayer, for its simplicity and honesty; and he compared the stiff alignment of objects with the devout arrangement of flowers on an altar.

37 DIEGO VELÁZQUEZ (1599–1660). Spanish. *The Adoration of the Magi.* Dated on the stone at the Virgin's feet, *1619* (read *1617* by some scholars). Oil on canvas, 79⅞ x 49¼"

The figures in *The Adoration of the Magi,* painted when he was twenty, seem strikingly individual, and recall Velázquez' early *bodegones*—pictures showing people cooking or eating in low-class inns, painted with extraordinary verisimilitude. Indeed, some authorities (including the catalogue of the Prado) see these figures as portraits of Pacheco, his daughter Juana de Miranda whom Velázquez had already married, and the artist himself.

The basis of the claim is unclear, but in any case the natural types and costumes here used by Velázquez were an innovation. The modeling is strong and correct and achieved with broad strokes of heavy paint—the technical antithesis of the artist's famous late works. The landscape is very dark, but effective with its tree forms and mountain silhouetted against a clear yellow sky. The colors of the figures also are contrasted with the dark landscape, the Virgin's kerchief being a luscious pink. An early lithographic copy of the picture shows the canvas as having been wider, and thus the figures at either side must have originally seemed less cramped.

38 DIEGO VELÁZQUEZ (1599–1660). Spanish. *The Venerable Mother Jerónima de la Fuente.* Signed: *diego Velazquez f. 1620.* Oil on canvas, 63 x 43¼"

233

At the very top of the canvas is inscribed: *Bonum est prestolari cum silentio salutare Dei* ("It is a good and wholesome thing to listen to God in silence"). Around the good Mother Jerónima's crucifix is a partly legible flying label, and there are additional inscriptions on either side of her feet, giving her name and convent.

Seldom has a painter brought us closer to the presence of a severe and dedicated old religious. At the age of sixty-five, in 1620—the year this picture was painted—Mother Jerónima left Spain to found a convent of Franciscan nuns in Manila. According to Ortega y Gasset, this was "the first convent of Franciscan nuns in the New World." Interested as Franciscan nuns always are in the embroidery of church vestments and the making of lace for altar-cloths, it is a fairly safe surmise that this convent was the first to encourage the production of that very delicate embroidery on pineapple cloth which is known to have been taught in the Philippines by the Spanish nuns. Called simply "Philippine embroidery," it was imported into Spain for years, perhaps for centuries.

This painting was purchased in 1944 by the National Ministry of Education from the nuns of Mother Jerónima's old convent of Santa Isabel de los Reyes, in Toledo. Earlier, it was thought by the nuns to have been painted by Luis Tristán, but cleaning in 1926 revealed Velázquez' signature and the date.

39 Diego Velázquez (1599–1660). Spanish. *Prince Baltasar Carlos in Hunting Dress*. Painted 1635–36. Oil on canvas, 75¼ x 40½"

In this picture we see again, as in the portrait of Baltasar Carlos on his pony (plate 28), the alert eyes, the firm mouth, and the erect posture of the little Prince, but without the babyish pseudo-majesty of the earlier portrait. Here Velázquez shows the Prince, six years old as the inscription informs us (*Anno Aetatis Suae VI*), grown to be a real boy. Clad in correct hunting costume of green cap, white lace collar, and dark suit, he holds an arquebus negligently in his gloved hand—an arquebus that has been identified as one given to his father, Philip IV, when he was a boy, by the Viceroy of Navarre. At the feet of Prince Carlos lies a heavy bird dog, and at the right of the picture a greyhound, or rather, a part of one, for the canvas has evidently been narrowed at the right by several inches. Indeed, an old copy of the painting even shows a second greyhound. The landscape behind the Prince, with its lowering clouds, seems to foreshadow good hunting weather. The tree at the right with its overhanging branches, the distant Guadarramas with a lightening of the clouds behind them, add greatly to the pictorial quality of the picture. Appropriately, this portrait once hung in the royal hunting lodge, the Torre de la Parada.

40 Diego Velázquez (1599–1660). Spanish. *St. Anthony the Abbot and St. Paul the Hermit.*

Painted about 1640. Oil on canvas, 101¼ x 74"

This picture is one of the most immediately lovable of all those by Velázquez. First one appreciates the figures of the two good and simple old men devoutly expressing their gratitude to God for the double portion of bread which the raven is flying in. (The bird, which had been in the habit of bringing daily nourishment to St. Paul, considerately increased the ration when the hermit was visited by St. Anthony.) But almost more prepossessing is the landscape in which the two saints are seen: the graceful tree with its delicate bluish foliage open to the silvery light, the happy blue sky and white clouds, the road leading the eye off through the pleasant valley, and finally, giving seriousness and weight to it all, the great central rock.

The story is told in the old episodic manner of the Middle Ages. St. Anthony in his black habit was determined to know the ancient hermit St. Paul before he was taken by death. The picture shows him on this long journey asking the way of a centaur and of a satyr, and at last, under the rock, knocking at the gate of the old man's cave. The visit was not a long one, for St. Paul's strength was ebbing. Before many days he died. But poor St. Anthony too was old and tired, too tired to bury the body of his new friend. However two lions, who were fond of the deceased, came and dug his grave.

There has been much disagreement as to the period in which Velázquez painted this picture. Enrique Lafuente's opinion seems most reasonable. The similarity is noted between this landscape and the lovely one in the portrait of the Count-Duke of Olivares at the Battle of Fuenterrabia (1638). In fact the style in the landscape of the two hermits is even farther developed.

The picture was commissioned from the artist by Queen Isabella, the first wife of Philip IV, for the Hermitage of St. Paul in the Buen Retiro.

41 Diego Velázquez (1599–1660). Spanish. *The Coronation of the Virgin*. Painted about 1641. Oil on canvas, 69¼ x 48⅞"

This handsome work, painted almost entirely in positive rose pink, blue, and reddish purple, reveals in the heads of God the Father and God the Son the same sort of free, thin brushwork as that which the artist used in his picture of Sts. Anthony and Paul (plate 40). It was painted on the order of Queen Isabella (Isabel de Borbón) for the chapel in her apartment in the Alcázar. This type of Coronation in which the Virgin receives the crown, in this instance a wreath of roses, from the entire Trinity, gathered together in a sky radiant with bright clouds, had been treated in much the same way by El Greco some thirty-five years earlier on an oval canvas for the Hospital de la Caridad at Illescas, and it is probable that the Queen had seen this painting by El Greco or one of the replicas, and wished to have one of the same subject by Velázquez. The type of the Virgin, lovely and self-contained, may have been

influenced by the work of the superlative Sevillian sculptors in wood, Martínez Montañés and Alonso Cano.

42 Diego Velázquez (1599–1660) and Juan Bautista Martinez del Mazo (1612–1667). Spanish. *View of Saragossa*. Painted 1646–47. Oil on canvas 71¼ x 130¼"

Mazo, who had some indeterminate part in this painting, was born near Cuenca and came to Madrid as a youth to study with Velázquez. By the age of twenty-one he seems to have finished his apprenticeship and to have married Velázquez' daughter Francisca. He must have had a remarkable talent, but among critics there is little agreement as to just what he painted. Early in 1644 he was appointed a Painter to the King, and soon after was made drawing master to young Prince Baltasar Carlos.

In April, 1646 the King and Baltasar Carlos set off with attendants on a tour of Navarre and Aragon. They remained for some time in Pamplona because the Prince fell ill. While there, the royal lad ordered his painter, Mazo, to render a view of the fortified castle of Pamplona and the surrounding countryside, showing in the foreground local people performing Basque dances. The painting is lost, but the existing copy of it in the Duke of Wellington's collection, though of poor quality, reveals Mazo as an admirable composer of landscape. When the royal party finally moved on to Saragossa, the Prince ordered Mazo to paint that city from a point on the other side of the Ebro. The Prince's health grew worse, and he died on October 9, just short of the age of seventeen years.

The *View of Saragossa* showing the two Cathedrals, the Exchange, and other fine buildings bathed in a glowing luminosity, is given further vivacity by numerous people gathered on the nearer bank. When Mazo returned to Madrid and thence again to Pamplona, he asked a learned friend to compose the Latin inscription which is found at the lower left corner: "At the command of the puissant King Philip of Spain, Mazo put the last brush strokes to the city of Saragossa in 1647." Of Mazo, the art-historian Palomino wrote (1715–24), "He painted hunting subjects admirably and also views of cities." When Velázquez died in 1660, Mazo was nominated First Painter. Did he paint Saragossa, or did he paint only the figures in the foreground? Some critics think the city was beyond his powers, some the figures. And the *Fountain of the Tritons* and the allied dark and emotional landscapes which hang in the Prado? Quite possibly he painted all of them (excepting of course the inspired little views at the Villa Medici), and that would make him one of history's finest landscape painters.

43 Diego Velázquez (1599–1660). Spanish. *The Surrender of Breda* (detail of plate 27)

The two central figures in the famous picture are probably unsurpassed in their expression of *gentileza*, or noble magnanimity. Justin of Nassau surrenders the key of the city of Breda with a look of respect uncontaminated with humility, and Spínola in resting his armored hand on the shoulder of the defeated Dutch general expresses a friendliness which has remained alive despite eight months of the unrelenting hardship and pressure of a siege.

44 Diego Velázquez (1599–1660). Spanish. *Queen Mariana of Austria.* Painted 1652–53. Oil on canvas, 91 x 51⅝"

Mariana of Austria was a daughter of Philip IV's sister, Maria of Hungary (whom Velázquez had painted at Naples in 1630). She had been betrothed to Prince Baltasar Carlos, but the young Prince died in 1646, the same year in which Mariana's mother died, and Philip claimed her as his new bride, for he had been two years a widower. Three more years elapsed, however, before the child arrived in Spain, where she became Queen before she had reached the age of fifteen.

In her portraits she looks as though she had never laughed, but tradition tells us that once when she first came to Spain she shouted with amusement at some buffoonery and was severely informed that queens did not laugh in public. Her first child, the Infanta Margarita, gave her trouble at birth, and at least three years passed after her marriage before she could sit to Velázquez for this portrait. Sánchez Cantón calls it "one of the most important examples of the technical excellence which this artist achieved."

Mariana's life was less happy than many, for her second child, the Infante Felipe Prosper, born in 1657, was puny and never reached the age of four years, and her third, the famous Charles II, called "the Bewitched," born in 1661, was woefully subnormal. Mariana was about thirty years younger than her husband, and she survived him by about as many.

45 Diego Velázquez (1599–1660). Spanish. *Queen Mariana of Austria* (detail of plate 44)

The French Impressionists derived from Velázquez and Goya much of what they introduced into the modern technique of painting. The brilliant portrait of Queen Mariana, painted by Velázquez in 1652 or 1653, after his return from the second of his visits to Italy, reveals some of the discoveries that he had made in expressing the alive, quivering, almost unraveled appearance of solid objects under the influence of light. A typical example is the rendition of Mariana's flaccid left hand which holds her enormous handkerchief. Not only the fingers but also the jeweled rings, bracelet, and cuff are tremulous with light.

46 Diego Velázquez (1599–1660). Spanish. *The Spinners* ("*Las Hilanderas*") or *The Fable of Arachne.* Painted about 1657. Oil on canvas, 84⅝ x 113¾"

This marvelously interesting work, painted toward the end of Velázquez' life, has always been profoundly admired as perhaps the artist's greatest technical achievement, yet its true subject matter has been understood only in recent years, and then only through the successive contributions and discoveries of three separate scholars, Enriqueta Harris, Diego Angulo Iñiguez, and María Luisa Caturla.

The story is that of Minerva and Arachne, as Ovid gives it in *The Metamorphoses.* Arachne, a girl of humble birth, became famous throughout Lydia for her skill in weaving. Reports of her accomplishment and her self-congratulation reached the ears of Minerva, the goddess who presided over the weaver's art. She appeared in Arachne's rooms and challenged her to a contest. Minerva thereupon wove pictures illustrating the dire punishments which the gods had visited upon brash mortals. Arachne responded by illustrating the follies of mighty Jove, Minerva's father, including the story of his disguising himself as a bull in order to deceive Europa. Hers was a rare feat of weaving, and an insult to the gods. Minerva, in a fury, put a rope around Arachne's neck and, changing her into a spider, cried, "Live, guilty woman, but hang and continue to hang and spin through all future time!"

Velázquez is said to have used the Santa Isabel tapestry repair shop in Madrid as his setting. In the lower workroom five women are spinning and winding yarn. In the strongly lighted upper room are three ladies of Lydia, come to witness the contest. Helmeted Minerva with raised arm utters her curse, and Arachne stands before her woven picture of *The Rape of Europa*—actually a copy after the painting by Titian, which was then still in Spain (now in the Isabella Stewart Gardner Museum, Boston).

The painting of the fable of Arachne was not made by Velázquez for the King, but for his Honorary Huntsman (*Montero de Cámara*), Pedro de Arce, in whose inventory of 1664 its listing under its correct title was discovered by María Luisa Caturla. It did not appear in the royal inventories until the eighteenth century.

47 Diego Velázquez (1599–1660. Spanish. *The Spinners* ("*Las Hilanderas*") or *The Fable of Arachne* (detail of plate 46)

In this half-lighted part of his picture, Velázquez reveals the wonderful effectiveness of his loose, free brush strokes. The perfect impression that one receives of the whirring wheel has been remarked by Sánchez Cantón; the beauty of the old woman's kerchief, and the racy and authentic personality of the girl carrying the bundle, are equally noteworthy. To appreciate the perfection of the composition one need only try to imagine the elimination of any item, for every point of light, every fold and shadow, every stick contributes to the interest of the part and to the expressiveness of the whole.

48 Diego Velázquez (1599–1660). Spanish. *Philip IV Aged about Fifty.* Painted about 1655. Oil on canvas, 27⅛ x 22"

In this portrait the mature Philip wears a black costume with a white *golilla,* the stiff, outstanding collar which had first been introduced in Spain when Philip was about twenty. The King looks somewhat worn for his age, but historians tells us there were reasons of a military and political sort. The expulsion of the *Moriscoes* continued to sap the economy; and recently, after sixty years of Spanish suzerainty, Portugal in 1640 had regained her independence. There had been the rebellion in Naples led by Masaniello, and similar upsets in Catalonia. The trusted minister Olivares had to be expelled from court in 1643, coinciding with the disastrous battle of Rocroy, considered to mark the decline of Spanish military power in Europe; and finally the Peace of Westphalia in 1648 had made all the Spanish losses cruelly manifest.

A version of this portrait in the National Gallery, London, is thought to be a replica of the Prado one, or rather a studio copy, partly by Velázquez. There the King wears the badge of the Golden Fleece.

49 Francisco Goya y Lucientes (1746–1828). Spanish. *The Witches' Sabbath.* Painted 1819–23. Mural transferred to canvas, 55⅛ x 172½"

Before withdrawing to France, there to spend the last part of his life, Goya lived a few years in a modest, two-story house near the Segovia bridge, across the Manzanares from Madrid. It was given the appropriate name of Deaf Man's Villa (*la Quinta del Sordo*), and it was there that the old man covered the plaster walls with fourteen of the weirdest paintings of his entire career, the famous "Black Pictures." Goya painted them almost entirely in lampblack, white, and earth-brown. Downstairs in the dining room the upper part of two opposite fifteen-foot walls were filled, one with *The Holiday Picnic* (*La Romeria*), showing a guitarist surrounded by crazy listeners, and the other with *The Witches' Sabbath,* here reproduced.

This picture shows the Devil, disguised as a goat clad in a monk's cassock, preaching his evil sermon to the wildest looking lot of low-grade women ever painted. Only one woman has a chair to sit on. She wears a proper mantilla, carries a muff, and is evidently a silly lady who has strayed into very strange company indeed.

In a sense the nightmares on the walls came true. Ferdinand VII imported French soldiery to support him in abrogating the semi-liberal Constitution. The dogs of reactionary absolutism were unleashed, and the police threw thousands of known constitutionalists into prison. It was the familiar pattern, and Goya, largely because of the political dynamite in some of his prints, was officially listed as a subversive citizen. On September 17, 1823 he gave his *Quinta del Sordo,* or

235

the portion of it owned by him, to his grandson, Mariano Goya. An influential royal appointee, José Duaso, took Goya into his own house and kept him in hiding for several months. In the spring of 1824, at the age of seventy-eight, he managed to get permission to visit France, "for the sake of his health."

In 1873 Baron Emil von Erlanger, a German banker, bought the *Quinta del Sordo,* had the Black Pictures transferred from the walls to canvas, and later gave them to the Prado.

50 DIEGO VELÁZQUEZ (1599–1660). Spanish. *A Garden at the Villa Medici, Rome* (detail of plate 30)

When seen at a little over actual size, this typical portion of Velázquez' remarkably advanced painting, evidently done *con amore,* shows how thinly and simply the paint was applied to the canvas. The classical bust (Homer?) at the right is drawn with the fewest possible strokes in light color on top of the dark mass. Are the two casual men visitors at the Villa, or contractors in charge of the repair work?

51 DIEGO VELÁZQUEZ (1599–1660). Spanish. *Self-Portrait* (detail of *The Maids of Honor,* plate 31)

The ingratiating portrait at the age of fifty-seven that he made of himself at work on the painting *The Maids of Honor* is the only likeness of Velázquez which can be accepted without hesitation. The red cross of the Order of Santiago shown as if embroidered on his front was not painted by the artist himself, but was ordered by the King, after the death of Velázquez—even painted by the King's own hand, according to some reports. From 1658 on, Velázquez, perhaps at the King's suggestion, had made application for a knighthood of the Order of Santiago and offered evidence from distinguished friends to prove that he had always conducted himself like a noble. As a result of the King's request direct to the Pope, the application was finally granted at the end of November, 1659.

In the following spring the King undertook an expedition of the Court to meet Louis XIV on the Isle of Pheasants at the French border for the betrothal of the French monarch to Philip's charming-looking daughter, María Teresa. Velázquez as Palace Chamberlain was responsible for all arrangements, and the effort left him exhausted. Thus he contracted an illness, and died on August 6, 1660, having had little time to enjoy his right to wear the cross of Santiago.

52 ALONSO CANO (1601–67). Spanish. *The Virgin with the Effulgence.* Painted about 1630–40. Oil on canvas, 64⅛ x 42⅞"

Alonso Cano appears to have had a career as stormy as that of the romantic and passionate Italian Caravaggio. He was an Andalusian, born in Granada, but as a youth he moved with his father to Seville and entered the studio of Pacheco, the master and father-in-law of Velázquez. He became a sculptor and architect as well as a painter and received instruction from the Mannerist painters Juan del Castillo and the elder Herrera, and from the sculptor Juan Martinez Montañéz. He was forced to flee from Seville in 1637 because he had severely wounded another painter in a brawl, and going to Madrid, was introduced at Court and became drawing teacher to Prince Baltasar Carlos.

The suspicion that he had murdered his second wife sent him off to Valencia, and it must have been native temperament rather than the hot blood of youth which kept him in perpetual discord, for when he was over fifty he was still giving offence to ecclesiastics and laymen. The last seven years of Cano's life were spent in Granada, where he held the post of chief architect of the Cathedral.

Most of Caravaggio's paintings look like the work of an uproarious man, but nothing of Cano's turbulent life disturbs *The Virgin with the Effulgence,* so called from the small area of light behind her head that resembles a moon veiled by clouds. The color is delicate, and the blue sky over the group soft and hazy. The Virgin sits on a rock, and behind her the grassy rolling pastures are turning green with spring rains. The serious mien of the Madonna as she gazes at her sleeping blond Child is a reminder that this theme of the slumbering Infant was often associated with the Pietá. Clasping her sleeping Son, the Virgin is troubled by forebodings of His Passion and the sorrowful day when she will similarly hold on her lap the lifeless body of the crucified Christ.

53 JUAN CARREÑO DE MIRANDA (1614–85). Spanish. *Charles II.* Painted 1673. Oil on canvas, 79⅛ x 55½"

The sharp descent from Velázquez to Carreño, who succeeded him as Court Painter, is paralleled by the sorry succession from King Philip IV, who died in 1665, to his son Carlos II, known as *El Hechizado,* or "the Bewitched." Don Juan Carreño de Miranda was the son of an aristocratic Asturian family, and was brought when young to Madrid to study painting there. His earlier life was devoted to the painting of large religious frescoes in the churches of Madrid and Toledo, ambitious, complicated, but disappointing compositions in which he yet revealed himself a painter aware of the artistic currents of his time. He copied portraits by Velázquez, and only after the great painter's death did Carreño come into a position of any prominence. An old chronicler records that Carlos II, whom he painted many times, esteemed him highly and was deeply moved by his death.

It is difficult to conceive of any human feelings in the breast of this bizarre figure, the last of the Hapsburg kings. He had been born to Philip and his young wife Mariana of Austria in November of 1661, the very year of the sad death at the age of four of their little son Felipe Prosper. Philip himself died when Carlos was not quite four years old, and so the widow became regent for her infant son until he came of age in 1679. Though Carlos was married twice, to Marie Louise of Orléans and to Mariana of Neuburg, he had no heirs, but appointed as his successor the grandson of the Sun-King Louis XIV of France, thus bringing the Bourbon rule to the Spanish throne. In this portrait painted in 1673 Carreño posed the young King in the Hall of Mirrors of the Alcázar, resting his hand on one of the console tables supported by lions which are still to be seen in the Prado and in the Royal Palace in Madrid. The position of the hands and feet wanly recalls the great dignified portraits of Philip which Velázquez made when he first went to work at the court.

54 BARTOLOMÉ ESTEBAN MURILLO (1618–82). Spanish. *A Galician Girl with a Coin.* Painted about 1645–50. Oil on canvas, 24¾ x 16⅞"

Bartolomé Esteban Murillo, perhaps the most popular of Spanish painters, was an Andalusian and spent almost all of his life in Seville. Like Cano, he studied there with Juan del Castillo, and his early pictures give little promise of the richness and warmth that characterize the works for which he is known and loved. A perceptible broadening and increase of power in coloring and luminosity in the work of his middle twenties has led critics to assume that he made a trip to Madrid in 1642–44 and benefited by studying the works of Rubens, Van Dyck, Correggio, and Titian which he saw there.

In his youth he was especially fond of painting peasant types, very credible though sentimentalized ragamuffins eating melons or grapes; in his mature works, the sweetly sympathetic and appealing Virgins of the Immaculate Conception or the glowing generous figures of the Virgin and Child, he never loses his touch with human beings.

The Galician peasant girl falls into the same category as his paintings of ragged Andalusian boys. In her broad cheekbones and widely parted lips Murillo has put a look of good nature and docility that accords with the character that Spaniards customarily ascribe to Galicians. Galicia is the breathtakingly picturesque and rugged region in the northwest corner of Spain, bounded on the west by the stormy Atlantic and on the south by Portugal. The influence of the robust Portuguese and the necessity of forcing a living from an obdurate and unsmiling land have stamped the Galicians with a different character from the passionate and fiery Spaniards of other regions. All of this has gone into Murillo's generalized but truthful painting of the *Galician Girl with a Coin.*

55 BARTOLOMÉ ESTEBAN MURILLO (1618–1682). Spanish. *Rebecca and Eliezer.* Painted about 1650. Oil on canvas, 42⅛ x 67⅜"

As we read in Genesis 24, when Abraham was well along in years, he became concerned about a suitable wife for his son Isaac, who had been given to him and Sarah in their old age. He did not want her to be a girl from Canaan, where he was then living, but from his own country and kin in Mesopotamia. He accordingly sent Eliezer, his chief servant, to seek the bride.

Eliezer with his ten camels arrived at the city of his master's kinsmen "at the time of the evening, the time that women go out to draw water." Praying to the Lord to prosper his mission, he resolved to elect the young woman who would respond graciously to his request for a drink of water and would give water to his camels also. Standing by the fountain, he saw Rebecca come out, and "the damsel was very fair to look upon." She filled her pitcher, and he ran to meet her, putting his plea to her as he had planned. She not only gave him drink, but "drew for all his camels" and, questioning her, Eliezer discovered that she was the grandchild of Abraham's brother, and decided that she was the woman whom the Lord had appointed for his master's son. The next day, with the consent of her family she journeyed back to Canaan with Eliezer and was warmly welcomed by her bridegroom Isaac.

In this delightfully blond and luminous painting, Murillo has shown four comely girls with their pitchers at the well. Rebecca, the one whose face reveals the greatest depth of feeling and the finest character, holds the pitcher for Eliezer to drink his fill, before the thirsty camels, grouped at the far left, receive their portion. Rebecca's modestly averted glance suggests that charity is not a new experience to her, and she alone of the four seems unaware of the portent of the casual meeting with the stranger at the well.

56 BARTOLOMÉ ESTEBAN MURILLO (1618–82). Spanish. *The Immaculate Conception*. Painted about 1665–70. Oil on canvas, 81⅛ x 56¾″

The dogma of the Immaculate Conception, which holds that the Virgin Mary was conceived and born without taint of original sin, was warmly revered in Spain, especially in the south, in Seville, where Murillo worked. Though the belief had been popularly cherished for many years, it did not receive official sanction by the Church until Murillo's lifetime, when Pope Alexander VII issued an ordinance in its favor.

The newly established doctrine found in Murillo an enthusiastic propagator, and no artist's name has been more closely associated with this subject than his. The crescent moon on which the Virgin stands in representations of the Immaculate Conception, and the stars that often form a halo about her head, are due to her partial identification with the Woman of the Apocalypse, whom St. John saw in his vision on the island of Patmos: "A great wonder in heaven; a woman clothed with the sun, and the moon under her feet, and upon her head a crown of twelve stars." It was established that she should wear a white tunic and a blue mantle; her long hair hangs free, and there is always a strong emphasis on youth and purity in her

facial expression and demeanor. In this version by Murillo, known as the "Escorial Conception," cherubs throng the glory about the Virgin's head, and chubby little angels billow in the clouds about her feet, bearing white lilies, roses, and branches of palm and olive.

Murillo's skill in designing the picture, the beautiful upward thrust of the lines of the composition, and the simple outline of the figure silhouetted against the glowing light, lead to the conclusion that he painted it late in his career, about 1665-70, not long before his famous large paintings in the Hospital of the Caridad in Seville, *Moses Striking Water from the Rock* and *The Multiplication of the Loaves and Fishes.*

57 BARTOLOMÉ ESTEBAN MURILLO (1618–82). Spanish. *St. Anne Teaching the Virgin*. Painted about 1660. Oil on canvas, 86¼ x 65″

In this painting Murillo gives an exceptionally human and credible rendering of a popular theme. He has clothed both figures in costumes worn in seventeenth-century Seville. The youthful Virgin has the look of a highly intelligent pupil, and St. Anne is full of benevolence and character. The composition is simple and strong, the light falling sharply upon the bold folds of the costumes and on the sewing basket at the left.

Enriqueta Harris, writing of this picture, calls attention to objections to this beloved subject made by Velázquez' teacher, Pacheco. In his *Arte de la Pintura* (1649), he wrote that since the Virgin had full use of her reason from the beginning, and since the suggestion that she could take lessons from anyone would argue imperfection, any painter of this subject must be involved in error. Pacheco at the time was an adviser to the Inquisition, but the subject of the Education of the Virgin was highly popular, and Murillo, like the devoutly Catholic Rubens who painted it too, remained unharmed.

58 FRANCISCO GOYA Y LUCIENTES (1746–1828). Spanish. *The Snowstorm*. Painted 1786. Oil on canvas, 108¼ x 115⅜″

Three men carrying packs and muffled in capes and blankets are struggling afoot across mountains against cold wind and falling snow. They are leading a mule laden with a slaughtered pig, and are escorted by a soldier and a hooded man with a gun. This picture of typical Spanish life is one of the sixty-three cartoons for tapestries which Goya painted for the royal tapestry factory of Santa Barbara between 1775 and 1792. Forty-four are now in the Prado. This one, representing *The Snowstorm*, according to the factory's account books was delivered toward the end of the year 1786. By that time the painter Raphael Mengs had left Spain, and Francisco Bayeu, Goya's brother-in-law, was in charge of the factory. The tapestry woven after Goya's *Snowstorm* was intended for the Royal Palace at El Pardo near Madrid, and is actually now conserved there.

59 FRANCISCO GOYA Y LUCIENTES (1746-1828). Spanish. *The Flower Girls*. Painted 1786. Oil on canvas, 109 x 75⅝″

In the fresh springlike countryside, with a tree reminiscent of Tiepolo's decorations at the Villa Valmarana in Vicenza, Italy, a simply dressed young woman is leading a child by the hand. A second girl, kneeling gracefully, offers her flowers which she has picked, and a foolish manservant attempts to startle the first young woman with a baby rabbit. The picture is the last word in innocent genre painting. Like *The Snowstorm*, delivered in the same year, it was painted for the Santa Barbara tapestry factory. The tapestry woven from this cartoon was not completed until two years later. Only one example was woven, and it went into the dining room in the Palace at El Pardo. A set of paintings of *The Four Seasons*, only about thirteen inches high, was ordered from Goya by the Duke and Duchess of Osuna. All were based on his tapestry cartoons, *The Flower Girls* representing Spring, *The Snowstorm* (plate 58) representing Winter, and two other famous cartoons representing Summer and Autumn.

60 FRANCISCO GOYA Y LUCIENTES (1746–1828). Spanish. *The Flower Girls* (detail of plate 59)

From this charming detail alone, it would be crystal clear that Goya delighted in pretty women as well as in juicy paint. Although seen almost in rear view, the flowergirl's youth and sweet enthusiasm are evident. Her skin is smooth and fresh, but in her costume Goya permits himself to load on the creamy paint, making a strong appeal to the sense of touch.

61 FRANCISCO GOYA Y LUCIENTES (1746–1828). Spanish. *Doña Tadea Arias de Enríquez*. Painted 1790–95. Oil on canvas, 74¾ x 41¾″

This attractive young lady, standing beside a large urn in her garden and pulling on her long glove, represents Goya's urbane and delicate eighteenth-century style of portraiture. The sheer white dress is underlaid with a pink foundation, and the jewelry and trimming are black like her elaborately dressed hair. Goya was paid 10,000 reales for it.

The noted student of Goya, A. de Beruete y Moret, remarks, "This Doña Tadea speaks in Spanish" and characterizes her as "a lovely and sympathetic person." But her pretty face does not wear the noncommital expression of fashionable portraits by, for instance, Mengs or Vigée Le Brun. It clearly expresses a fixed intention of some sort, and a patience which one had better not try too far.

62 FRANCISCO GOYA Y LUCIENTES (1746–1828). Spanish. *General José de Urrutia*. Painted 1798. Signed

237

lower right: *Goya al general Urrutia.*
Oil on canvas, 78¾ x 53⅛"

A prime example, this, of what Sánchez Cantón calls Goya's "implacable representation of faces." Urrutia (1739-1803), by birth a Basque from the province of Viscaya, conducted a successful campaign in 1793 against the French in the mountainous border provinces. He was appointed Captain-General two years later after the second Treaty of Basel, the international agreement for which the Minister Manuel Godoy was given credit and styled Prince of the Peace.

But Urrutia was soon at loggerheads with Godoy, and his career ended. The war in which he distinguished himself had been brought on by the Spanish king, Charles IV, who resented the treatment which the French Revolution had accorded his kinsman Louis XVI, and hoped that his armies in the Pyrenees could stop demoralizing French ideas from crossing the mountains into Spain.

63 FRANCISCO GOYA Y LUCIENTES (1746–1828). Spanish. *The Colossus.* Painted about 1820. Oil on canvas, 45⅝ x 41⅜"

An entire village including its cattle is scattering in a wild panic because a mountain-high, nude giant has appeared nearby, sitting on the ground yet towering above the clouds. He rests there, looking the other way, and as yet unaware of the terror he is causing. The only other creature that remains calm is a stupid donkey standing in the foreground.

In Sánchez Cantón's opinion, the technique indicates a date between 1808 and 1814, but some critics see a relation between *The Colossus* and the horrible nightmares of 1819 to 1823 that Goya painted on the walls of the *Quinta del Sordo.* Goya also made a fearful and wonderful aquatint known as *The Colossus,* in which the great creature sits brooding in a vast, empty landscape with no human object to compare him with for scale. Yet his hugeness is at once apparent. Although the print, like the painting, is undated and its date is in question, an inscription by Goya's son at least provides evidence that it was made after 1812.

64 FRANCISCO GOYA Y LUCIENTES (1746–1828). Spanish. *Self-Portrait.* Painted about 1817–19. Signed in upper part: *Fr. Goya. Aragonés. Por el mismo.* Oil on canvas, 18⅛ x 13¾"

Besides this remarkable self-revelation in paint, Goya made another, similar in scale, which belongs to the Academy of San Fernando, of which he was for many years a member. On the San Fernando example, the paint is loaded more heavily, the head and shoulders are placed at a sharp diagonal, and the date 1815 is clearly added to the signature.

The Prado's portrait shows our deaf friend still looking tough-fibered and alertly intelligent, but distinctly older than in the portrait

of 1815. The added years have made themselves evident principally in the mouth, the lips having at last relaxed a little, revealing the fatigue brought on by seventy-two years of living and working, twenty-five of them in a deaf man's world of silence.

65 FRANCISCO GOYA Y LUCIENTES (1746–1828). Spanish. *The Witches' Sabbath* (detail of plate 49)

Not far from the goat-disguised Evil One and directly in front of him at this nocturnal orgy sits the coarse-grained witch pictured in this detail. On her, especially, Goya has chosen to throw his lurid spotlight. In her excitement at this unholy occasion, her eyes are wildly staring with dread and greed, her thick lips are slackly apart, and the wide nostrils are distended, the unwashed embodiment of crude credulity and coarse sensuality.

66 FRANCISCO GOYA Y LUCIENTES (1746–1828). Spanish. *The Parasol.* Painted 1777. Oil on canvas, 41 x 59⅞"

According to the account books of the royal tapestry factory in Madrid, as analyzed by Sambricio, Goya's first cartoons were delivered in 1775 when he was already a mature man of twenty-nine years. Yet, judged by his figure drawing of that time, he had not yet matured as an artist. Two years later, however, when he delivered a pair of cartoons for tapestries destined as overdoors in the dining room of the Prince of Asturias at the Palace of El Pardo, he had gained far more skill, more understanding of the problems involved, and more comfortable self-assurance.

One of the subjects he designed showed a youth pouring wine down his gullet in a curving stream from a bottle held aloft, Spanish style. The mate to that design was *The Parasol,* an unusually pleasing group and simple enough to enable the tapestry to "carry" even when hung high above the eye level. The subject is merely a pretty young lady, brightly dressed, who rests on the ground beside a wall. A particularly absurd little dog sleeps on her lap, and a young *mozo* whom she has brought along as escort holds up a green parasol—which appears to afford more protection to his own arm than to his employer's person.

67 FRANCISCO GOYA Y LUCIENTES (1746–1828). Spanish. *The Family of Charles IV.* Painted 1800. Oil on canvas, 110¼ x 132¼"

In October, 1799, Goya was appointed First Painter to the King, and following closely upon this honor came the request that he portray the entire family on a single canvas. The idea may have been suggested by Louis Michel Van Loo's huge portrait of the family of Philip V, painted in 1743,

which shows about an equal number of people. But whereas Van Loo had almost all his royal personages spread out in armchairs among the architecture, Goya has his subjects standing in close formation.

The idea of portraying himself working at the canvas was doubtless suggested by Velázquez' *Maids of Honor* (plate 31). But in contrast with the disarming naturalness of that canvas, the arrangement by Goya, doubtless specified by the King, is stiffly official, with each member of the family wearing his or her court costume including every permissible decoration. The men and boys wear the blue and white ribbon of the Order of Charles III, and the ladies the ribbon of the Order of María Luisa. In the group at the left the youth in blue is the Prince (later, as Ferdinand VII, decidedly less prepossessing), and the lady averting her face is thought to typify his future betrothed —whose identity in 1800 was still undetermined.

In the center of the picture stands the Queen, holding onto her two youngest children, while the group at the right is led by the commonplace King, wearing a white wig and looking older than his fifty-one years. The mother at the right with an infant in arms is María Luisa, a daughter of the King and Queen, with her baby and its father, the Prince of Parma.

68 FRANCISCO GOYA Y LUCIENTES (1746–1828). Spanish. *The Family of Charles IV* (detail of plate 67)

The center of Goya's painting of *The Family of Charles IV* is not the King, for all his medals and foolish pomposity, but Queen María Luisa with her young children, one at each side. Napoleon, who saw her at Bayonne in 1808, is often quoted as having observed, "María Luisa has her past and her character written in her face, and it surpasses anything you dare imagine"; and in most portraits of her, the outrageousness of her brazen stare does indeed shock the beholder. Here in this stiff, official family portrait, however, she surprises us by her relaxation and good-nature as she places an affectionate right arm around the shoulders of her shy, eleven-year-old daughter, Doña María Isabel, whom she has dressed in a costume closely resembling her own.

69 FRANCISCO GOYA Y LUCIENTES (1746–1828). Spanish. *Maja Clothed.* Painted about 1796–98. Oil on canvas, 37⅜ x 74¾"

This canvas, with the *Maja Nude* (plate 70), constitutes a pair of paintings as famous and as fine as any of Goya's achievements. The two must have been painted about the same time as the joyous and earthy decorations in the dome of San Antonio de la Florida (1798), judging by their free execution. The earliest mention of them, however, is in 1808, when they were listed among the possessions of the First Minister, Manuel

238

Godoy. There they bore the titles, *A Gypsy Clothed* and *A Gypsy Nude*.

These paintings have afforded writers of popular biography and their readers much pleasurable titillation because of the legend that they represent Goya's wayward and enchanting sweetheart, the famous Duchess of Alba, and that the clothed *Maja* was painted under pressure in order to allay any suspicions which the nude *Maja* might have aroused in the Duke.

In actuality they were probably painted at least two years after the Duke's death, and in any case this broad-browed, wide-hipped woman with her level, appraising gaze, belonged to a physical type as far as possible from that of the Duchess of Alba, whose portraits agree in showing her bones small, her body slim, her face a narrow oval and her eyebrows heavy and strongly arched, creating an expression of enquiry.

As to the meaning of the often used word *maja,* each writer enjoys giving his own definition. A useful one would be: a pretty working-class girl with a gay spirit and a fondness for attractive clothes that conform to what her friends are wearing.

70 FRANCISCO GOYA Y LUCIENTES (1746–1828). Spanish. *Maja Nude.* Painted about 1796–98. Oil on canvas, 38⅛ x 74¾"

This beautiful pale nude was painted as a companion piece to the rosier *Maja Clothed* (plate 69) which shows the same young woman in the same pose. Although the pair belonged to Godoy, who owned a nude by Velázquez as well, it is not known whether they were painted for him. The pair did not reach the Prado until 1901, having been consigned along with many of the Titians and Rubenses to the comparative obscurity of the Academy of San Fernando as being too demoralizingly undressed.

71 FRANCISCO GOYA Y LUCIENTES (1746–1828). Spanish. *The Second of May, 1808.* Painted 1814–15. Oil on canvas, 104¾ x 135⅞"

When Napoleon decided to gobble up Spain, he tricked Charles IV and his heir to the throne, Prince Ferdinand, into meeting him on the French side of the border where they could be forced or induced to stay. Joseph Bonaparte was picked off another throne by his brother and set down on the throne of Spain. Naturally soldiers of the Imperial army had to be sent into Spain to assure success, with Egyptian cavalry (Mamelukes) to support them. "But the French discovered that Spain was a morsel easier swallowed than digested." On May 2, 1808, the Spanish people in Madrid courageously attacked with sticks, stones, and knives. Goya reports the scene with violence but without histrionics. The locale of the fight has usually been called the Puerta del Sol, but the Prado catalogue finds no resemblance to the buildings there.

Goya's interest in humanity knew no limits, but to horseflesh he seems to have paid little heed. Charles Poore noted this surprising limitation when he wrote that Goya's horses were "more epic than hippic."

The companion picture to *The Second of May* showing the horrors of the following day, is illustrated in the next plate.

72 FRANCISCO GOYA Y LUCIENTES (1746–1828). Spanish. *The Third of May, 1808.* Painted 1814–15. Oil on canvas, 104¾ x 135⅞"

The citizens of Madrid, unorganized and virtually unarmed, were no match for the French troops and within a few hours the heroic deeds of May 2 (see plate 71) had to cease. Then began the horrors, the awakening from a happy dream to methodical reality, as batches of suspects were taken by the troops to the hill near Prince Pio's house and shot.

It was not until the spring of 1814 that Goya received from the Regency the word to go ahead with the paintings with which he had proposed to illustrate Spain's "glorious insurrection against the tyrant of Europe." The commission was voted just in time, for the reactionary Ferdinand VII arrived home from France two weeks later.

73 FRANCISCO GOYA Y LUCIENTES (1746–1828). Spanish. *The Milkmaid of Bordeaux.* Painted about 1827. Oil on canvas, 29⅛ x 26¾"

In the spring of 1828 Goya died in Bordeaux at the age of eighty-two. His painting of *The Milkmaid* must have been painted at some time during his last year of life. It is one of his most humane and joyous pictures, and he put into it more modernity than into any other work. There she is, a simple, pretty young woman of the people, apparently sitting on her donkey and jogging along the street on her milk route. But the expression of living flesh and vital form through the use of divided color was scarely carried so far again until half a century later in the paintings of Renoir. This milkmaid must have amused Goya with her positive rules covering business transactions, for his housekeeper later reported that Goya had said, "This painting isn't obligated to give less than one ounce."

The Milkmaid is one of the more recent acquisitions of the Prado; it was a bequest of the Count of Muguiro in 1946.

74 VAN EYCK SCHOOL (Fifteenth Century). Flemish. *The Fountain of Living Water.* Painted about 1450. Oil on wood, 71¼ x 45⅝"

The figures, the grouping, and the mystical thought in this work at once suggest its similarity to *The Adoration of the Mystic Lamb,* the Van Eyck brothers' altarpiece in the Cathedral of St. Bavo in Ghent, which, finished in 1432, established the very foundation of Flemish painting. The "quality" in the Prado's elaborate panel, however—meaning the textures, the color, and the fineness of the drawing—are not up to the Van Eycks' standards, and thus it seems surely a somewhat later copy of a superlatively fine original. Judging by the symbolism, which goes back to sources in the twelfth and thirteenth centuries, the original was even earlier than the altarpiece of the Lamb; some scholars suppose it to have been painted between 1410 and 1420 (a date which would not exclude the Van Eycks, who were probably born in the late fourteenth century). Others, however, associate it with the journey made by Jan van Eyck to Spain in 1428–29.

The Prado panel must originally have been the central unit of a polyptych. The treatment of the subject, sometimes called *The Triumph of the Church over the Synagogue,* suggests a mystery play as its inspiration. On the upper platform beneath a Gothic baldacchino is Christ enthroned with the Sacrificial Lamb at his feet. At His right hand sits the Virgin Mary and on His left St. John the Evangelist reading his book of Revelation. On the middle plane are angels making music. One of them, at the right, holds a scroll with the text, in Latin, from the Song of Solomon: "A fountain of gardens, a well of living water." On a still lower plane, in the foreground of the picture, is a basin of water fed by a spring of the Water of Life, which issues from beneath the throne. On its surface float holy wafers, and groups of men are assembled at right and left. Those at the spectator's left (i.e., on the right hand of God) represent the hierarchy of the Church, with its pope in front, then its cardinal, its archbishop, its emperor, its king, its abbot, and others. Behind the king kneels the probable donor of the altarpiece. At the other side are the Jews, led by their high priest, broken, blindfolded, and confounded. A drawing exists of just such a group of defeated Jews, made in the style of the first quarter of the fifteenth century.

Two passages in the Revelation by St. John are appropriate: "For the Lamb which is in the midst of the throne shall feed them, and shall lead them unto living fountains of water" (Revelation 7:17); also, "And he shewed me a pure river of water of life, clear as crystal, proceeding out of the throne of God and of the Lamb" (Revelation 22:1).

The Prado's panel is probably the earliest Flemish painting to enter Spain. It is mentioned in 1454 in the Jeronimite monastery of El Parral in Segovia, a gift of Enrique IV of Castile, the brother of Isabella the Catholic.

75 ROGIER VAN DER WEYDEN (1400–64). Flemish. *The Pietà.* Painted 1440–50. Oil on wood, 18½ x 13¾"

Old documents refer to Rogier, when he was an apprentice, under the French form of Rogelet de le Pasture. He seems to have been a native of Tournai, and in 1427, at an unusually mature age, was formally apprenticed to Robert Campin. This painter (see plate 90) is now believed by most scholars to be identical with the one known as the Master of Flémalle, so called because one of his best paintings is thought to have come from a collection in a town of that name near Liége. Rogier, his most distinguished pupil, became a free master in 1432 and was made the official painter of Brussels by October of 1436. He died in that city in 1464.

Rogier, evidently endowed with an extraordinary sensitiveness to the most profound human emotions, developed early in his career a tense and nervous linear style perfectly adapted to the expression of deep religious feeling. Naturally he was attracted even more than the other artists of his time to themes concerned with the Passion of Christ.

This Prado *Pietà* is one of several replicas, variously ascribed to Rogier himself or to painters in his workshop, and in its solemn remoteness is perhaps the finest of them all. The spectator regards the moving scene as if he too were present, identifying himself with the reverent praying donor, of whom no more is known than his name of Broers, and the probability that he was a citizen of Malines.

76 ROGIER VAN DER WEYDEN (1400–64). Flemish. *The Pietà* (detail of plate 75)

The motif of the *Pietà* probably had its origin in the mystery plays, where late in the day, after the death of Christ on the cross, the Virgin took his body on her lap as she had once held him when he was an infant, and in lines which one such play assigned her, attempted to assuage her grief by momentarily increasing it.

The body of Christ, stiff in death, is blessedly past all feeling, in strong contrast with the Virgin who is suffering intense grief, and with St. John, who, though less abandoned, shows profound sadness.

77 Attributed to DIERIC BOUTS (about 1420–75). Flemish. *The Visitation.* Painted about 1450. Oil on wood, 31½ x 20⅞"

The Visitation is part of an ensemble consisting of four pictures arranged in a row. The subjects are traditional parts of the story of Christ's infancy: *The Annunciation, The Visitation, The Nativity,* (plate 93), and *The Adoration of the Magi* (plate 78). The Visitation, as recounted by St. Luke (1:36–56), is one of the very eloquent stories in that most eloquent Book of the New Testament. Elisabeth in her old age had miraculously become pregnant a few months since, and her cousin Mary, who had herself shortly before been visited by the Angel of the Annunciation, came to see the older woman. When Elisabeth saw Mary she cried out, "Blessed art thou among women, and blessed is the fruit of thy womb." And Mary in elation responded in the words of the *Magnificat:* "My soul doth magnify the Lord, and my spirit hath rejoiced in God my Savior."

These four fine and strong paintings are officially ascribed in the Prado catalogue to Dieric Bouts, but the attribution is not positive. Although the great authority on Netherlandish painting, Max J. Friedländer, lists

them (in *Die Alt-niederlandische Malerei,* Vol. III) as the earliest known works of Bouts, he notes an unusual direct frontal lighting with curiously simplified modeling, and frankly admits that "this is not a style which can be found anywhere else" in Bouts' work. The author of the four paintings was in fact almost certainly Aelbert van Ouwater, who like Bouts was a native of Haarlem in the North Netherlands.

The one sure work by Van Ouwater, *The Raising of Lazarus,* painted about 1450 for St. Bavo's church in Haarlem, is now in the Museum at Berlin. Like Bouts and most other North European artists of his generation, Van Ouwater based his style on the great earlier Flemish masters in Bruges, Ghent, Tournai, and Brussels. His painting, however, remains a thing apart, for unlike Bouts, who as a young man had permanently abandoned Haarlem to settle in Tournai, Van Ouwater remained in the comparatively provincial city of his birth. His paintings—the definitely established *Raising of Lazarus* and also the Prado's *Infancy* panels, here ascribed to him —are far less highstrung than the paintings of Dieric Bouts. Where Bouts in general adhered to gaunt, puritanical types, Van Ouwater usually chose to paint placid "homey" faces with wide foreheads, his men including a great variety of types. More than once poor St. Joseph is made to appear so mild that the modeling of his face as well as the expression of his character seems diluted and flat.

78 Attributed to DIERIC BOUTS (about 1420–75). Flemish. *The Adoration of the Magi.* Painted about 1450. Oil on wood, 31½ x 20⅞"

"Now when Jesus was born in Bethlehem of Judaea in the days of Herod the King, behold, there came wise men from the east to Jerusalem. . . . And when they were come into the house, they saw the young child with Mary, his mother, and fell down, and worshipped him" (Matthew 2: 1–11).

This is the painting farthest to the right of the four which form the perhaps incomplete altarpiece ascribed to Bouts; but as we have argued in discussing *The Visitation* (plate 77) the panels were quite likely painted by his fellow townsman in Haarlem, Aelbert van Ouwater.

Writing in 1604, Van Mander mentions especially Van Ouwater's pleasing female figures; and in the Berlin *Raising of Lazarus* known to have been painted by him, the figures of Mary Magdalene and her sister Martha are lovely indeed. Lovelier still is the seated Virgin in this Epiphany scene. The clumsy and vigorous Christ Child reminds one more of babies by the Van Eycks than by Bouts, but it is Van Eyck uttered with a homely Hollandish accent.

79 Attributed to DIERIC BOUTS (about 1420–75). Flemish. *The Visitation* (detail of plate 77)

The early writer on Netherlandish art, Van Mander, laid especial stress on the fine land-

scapes painted by Aelbert van Ouwater. The detail reproduced here gives some idea of a landscape which we believe to be by him (see commentary for plate 77). The great age and goodness of this homespun Elisabeth is shown with touching affection and intimacy such as could hardly be found in the greater centers of art in Flanders and Brabant, yet entirely characteristic of mid-fifteenth-century art as developed in Holland.

80 HANS MEMLING (about 1433–94). Flemish. *The Adoration of the Magi.* Painted about 1470. Oil on wood, 37⅜ x 57⅛"

Hans Memling, one of the most approachable and attractive of the early Flemish painters, seems to have been born in Germany in the little town of Seligenstadt, near Frankfurt, and he must have gone to Flanders when quite young, for his art shows scarcely a trace of German influence. His way of composing pictures and the types he chose to paint suggest quite convincingly that he was a pupil of Rogier van der Weyden in Brussels, before he settled in Bruges in 1465.

But though he shows many similarities in form to the art of Rogier, the two painters could scarcely have been more unlike in temperament. The holy people in Memling's pictures are gentle and relaxed, posed in satisfyingly airy and balanced compositions, and his color is rich and mellow; and for Rogier's intense, quivering line he offers smooth, rounded surfaces.

In this *Adoration of the Magi,* the central panel of *The Three Kings* altarpiece, painted about 1470, Memling characteristically borrowed from and modified a work by his master; for in many elements it closely follows one of Rogier's great works, the Columba altarpiece in Munich, which has the same subject, similarly arranged, for its central panel. With Memling the entourage of the royal visitors presses less insistently into the small peaceful enclosure where the Virgin receives her guests, and the fervent reverence of Rogier's kneeling king is transformed into humble, hesitant affection.

About a decade after painting the Prado altarpiece, Memling made a smaller version for a donor named Jan Floreins. This little triptych, now in the Hospital of St. John in Bruges, is at once more intimate and more worldly, demonstrating admirably how Memling developed his own peculiar grace, as the example of his master Van der Weyden, who died in 1464, became increasingly remote.

81 HANS MEMLING (about 1433–94). Flemish. *The Nativity.* Painted about 1470. Oil on wood, 37⅜ x 23¾"

This *Nativity,* the left wing of *The Adoration of the Magi* (plate 80), is sometimes called *The Adoration of the Angels,* for a pair of diminutive creatures, much nearer in scale to the Holy Child than to his mother and St. Joseph, have come to join the Virgin as she marvels at the tiny naked form lying on her outspread cloak.

The suggestion has been made that Memling painted the altarpiece to which this panel belongs much earlier than 1470, while Rogier van der Weyden was still alive and Memling was working in his shop; but a warm, naive tenderness that is altogether Memling's own completely offsets the austerity which we associate with Rogier's treatment of the stone architecture. Here, more than in *The Adoration of the Magi*, he gives rein to his own inclinations, choosing for the Holy Mother a girlish type never found in works by Rogier, and imbuing the figure of the earnest St. Joseph, shielding his candle to symbolize a night scene, with a rapt and preoccupied air of responsibility for the Mother and Child whom he must protect.

82 HANS MEMLING (about 1433–94). Flemish. *The Nativity* (detail of plate 81)

A closer view of Memling's adoring Virgin reveals the fact that her very youthful appearance does not preclude a proper strength of character, a quality which Memling has subtly revealed in the mouth. Her hands, held open toward the newborn Child, express her wonder as well as her adoration, and appear to have been the artist's chief concern. As elaborately articulated and nervously complex in form and expression as any hands by his presumed master, Rogier van der Weyden, they are among the features which lead one to believe that the important triptych to which this *Nativity* belongs was painted relatively early in Memling's career.

83 HIERONYMUS BOSCH (about 1450–1516). Dutch. *A Child of Saturn* (exterior of *The Hay Wagon* triptych, closed; see plate 114). Painted about 1510. Oil on wood, 53⅛ x 35⅜"

Hieronymus Bosch was a native of 's-Hertogenbosch in North Brabant, Holland, a town somewhat off the beaten track, where Bosch spent his entire life. He was a unique artist, filling his pictures with grotesqueries and diableries, many representing Hell and its tortures, and others representing allegories which were easier for the artist's ordinary contemporaries to interpret than for scholars of the present day.

The Prado's triptych, *The Hay Wagon*, shows as its center, when open, a proverb well known in the sixteenth century (see plate 114). Its relation to this possibly later picture on the outer surfaces of the folded wings is unsolved. An independent painting by Bosch of the same wayfarer in the Boymans Museum, Rotterdam, is there entitled *The Prodigal Son*. Others have called the subject *The Peddler* or *The Road of Life*.

The clearest explanation is that recently published by Andrew Pigler (in *Burlington Magazine*, 1950, pp. 132–36), who points to fifteenth-century engravings by the Master E. S. and the Master of the Housebook, showing just such a vagabond beset by the

perils of the road, and labeled "Saturn." The Child of Saturn, according to astrologists, is beset by accidents, disasters, and violent death, for Saturn is the most malign of the planets. The saturnine person is of mean countenance and of melancholy, skeptical disposition, the sort of man dogs instinctively snarl at. Robberies, executions, lusts, quarrels, animals dead of violence or disease—these are his companions.

84 HIERONYMUS BOSCH (about 1450–1516). Dutch. *The Hay Wagon* (detail of plate 114)

This is a detail of the central panel of *The Hay Wagon* triptych (plate 114), so called because it illustrates an old Flemish proverb: "The world is a haystack; each plucks from it as much as he can get." The greedy struggle leads to inevitable quarrels. Here a middle-aged woman, wearing a black coif, perhaps that of some lay order, is attacking a rich, overfed peasant. The dry commentary on human types and human foibles takes a form later made familiar by the elder Pieter Bruegel, whose known production began about thirty-five years after Bosch had died.

85 GERARD DAVID (about 1450–1523). Flemish. *The Rest on the Flight into Egypt*. Painted about 1510. Oil on wood, 23⅝ x 15⅜"

The young and ladylike Virgin, not visibly travel-stained or weary, pauses in her journey to give nourishment to her beguiling and handsome little boy. A neat wicker hamper rests on the ledge of rock beside her, and far in the background, in the old-fashioned narrative style, they are shown again, and St. Joseph too, riding on donkeys through a deep wood. The trees rise tall and straight, the earth beneath them clean and bare of undergrowth as it still is in Flemish forests, and at the left there gleams through the trunks the golden light of the setting sun.

It is extraordinary how the best Flemish painters of the early period, though rigidly trained in the traditions of their craft and the technique of their masters and predecessors, managed on becoming mature artists to express with clarity their individual vision of the world and their personal interpretation of the Gospel.

Gerard David's paintings are consistently free from clumsiness and coarseness; even his torture scenes (of which there are several) show his predilection for physically refined and attractive people, moving with grace in whatever actions they are called upon to perform. This native taste for the exquisite may have been intensified in David by working as an illuminator. He was born in Oudewater, a little town near Gouda in the north Netherlands, and seems to have been educated in Haarlem, probably (like Geertgen tot Sint Jans, whose works his own early ones resemble) in the workshop of Aelbert van Ouwater. By 1484 he had moved south into Flanders, and we find him a member of the painters' guild in Bruges. There he was kept

busy for the ensuing three decades until his death. He came to know the great works by Jan van Eyck, Rogier van der Weyden, and Hans Memling, and the naïveté of his earlier works gave way to a mature style that was controlled and urbane, yet eloquent enough when the subject called for emotion. Like the other artists trained in the Haarlem tradition, he was a fine landscape painter. This is especially apparent in the paintings of *The Rest on the Flight*, a subject that he treated in the Prado's example and at least twice more with slight variations, in pictures at the Metropolitan Museum and the National Gallery, Washington.

86 BERNAERT VAN ORLEY (about 1492–1542). Flemish. *The Virgin of Louvain*. Painted about 1516. Oil on wood, 17¾ x 15⅜"

The youthful and graceful Virgin, tenderly clasping her Infant, is seated before an elaborate—and implausible—Northern version of Renaissance architecture. In a recessed opening beneath the platform on which she sits is a pot of roses, one of her attributes.

A label on the back of the panel bears an inscription which begins "*Johannes Mabeus Senat. P. Lov.*," adding an elaborate tribute to King Philip the Catholic and stating that the painting is presented to him. The traditional interpretation has been that it was Jan Mabuse, meaning Jan Gossaert of Maubeuge or Malbodius (the Latin form of the town's name), who painted the panel which the city of Louvain presented to Philip II. Sánchez Cantón of the Prado sees no reason for abandoning this reading of the inscription, but M. J. Friedländer and some other scholars believe that the initial words of the inscription refer to a Senator at Louvain by the name of Mabeus. In their opinion the style of the painting itself is that of Bernaert van Orley, early in his career. The occasion of the gift is thought to have been a tax abatement granted to Louvain in 1588 in consideration of a plague there ten years before.

Bernaert van Orley, born in Brussels in 1493, came of a noble family. In 1518 he was made Court Painter to Margaret of Austria, Regent of the Netherlands, and after 1530 continued in the same position under Margaret's successor, Mary of Hungary. Van Orley painted a number of fine altarpieces and other pictures, and his productions, together with those of Gossaert, are the chief examples of Italianized Flemish painting. He also furnished tapestry cartoons and designs for stained glass, some of which can now be found in Flemish churches. His early Madonnas show a strong influence of Raphael, whose cartoons for tapestries, woven in Brussels about 1515–19, Van Orley must have seen. An extremely careful painter, he tended to force vivacity into agitation and to overload his pictures with architecture.

87 JOACHIM PATINIR (about 1480–1524). Flemish. *The River Styx*. Painted about 1510. Oil on wood, 25¼ x 40½"

The longer one gazes at this picture, the more awesome it becomes, with its gleaming river reaching toward the far distant horizon, its illimitable landscape, and the utter loneliness of the frail bark that undertakes the fearful crossing. Small wonder that the naked figure cowering in the bow of the boat has hair standing on end, for not far off is the entrance to Pluto's palace toward which the ancient Charon is steering.

Charon—old, grim, and preoccupied—has no impulse to comfort his passenger, for thousands have passed this way, and he knows that there can be no comfort. At the arched entrance to the round tower can be seen Cerberus, the three-headed, serpent-tailed dog that guards the gate. He is friendly to those who enter but dangerous to those who would depart. At the left of the river are the Elysian Fields where angels stroll amidst park-like grounds studded with lakes, and beyond is a crystal building; in the far distance a town is visible. Over all float billowing white clouds bathed in a bright radiance.

But alas for the shrinking youthful passenger, the boat is not headed that way, and the dark shores of Tartarus are vastly forbidding. At the top of the entrance tower, swooning naked figures are being tortured, and in the distance frightful fires and billowing smoke suggest further tortures. It is easy to imagine the shrieks of the damned that reach the ears of the cowering passenger.

Joachim Patinir was born at Bouvignes, near Dinant, and must early have been impressed by the picturesquely rugged valley of the Meuse, which he recorded in strikingly original blue-green color gradations to express degrees of distance. In 1515 he bought the freedom of the Guild in Antwerp, and in the year 1520 he bought a house there, where Dürer visited him.

When, about the year 1510, Patinir in Antwerp was painting such emotional landscapes as *The River Styx*, with figures decidedly subordinated, he was initiating an important new sort of painting. At exactly the same time a German painter in the Danube valley, Albrecht Altdorfer, was boldly and independently embarked on the same new genre.

88 JOACHIM PATINIR (about 1480–1524). Flemish. *The Rest on the Flight into Egypt*. Painted about 1520. Oil on wood, 47⅝ x 69⅝"

In the right background of this painting Patinir illustrates a charming legend of the Madonna's flight. Herod's soldiers were following Mary, the Child, and Joseph, and Mary paused by a field that was being sown to grain. She said to the foremost peasant, "If men come asking for us, please say 'None passed since I sowed this grain.'" The next morning a miraculous field of golden grain greeted the happy peasant, who busied himself cutting the grain with his sickle. The soldiers arrived and in answer to their questions were told, "None came since I sowed this grain." So the soldiers gave up the pursuit and turned back.

This picture was painted about 1520; the figures were probably painted by Patinir himself, although he was famous as a landscape painter. Patinir often scattered small figures over his landscapes, but where important figures were called for he frequently engaged another painter to paint the figures (see plate 95). A famous lawsuit of the time decided that a master painter was only required by his contract to execute personally the flesh parts in his painting and might employ assistants for other parts such as draperies and landscapes. Patinir was in great demand to supply landscapes for the paintings of other artists. Although he did not actually invent landscape painting, his sweeping land views may be regarded as the foundation on which many landscape painters of the sixteenth and seventeenth centuries based their work.

89 JAN GOSSAERT (1478–about 1536). Flemish. *The Virgin and Child*. Painted about 1527. Oil on wood, 24¾ x 19⅝"

Jan Gossaert, called Mabuse, takes his nickname from his native town of Maubeuge in Hainaut. He was a free master in Antwerp by 1503 and soon afterward entered the service of Philip of Burgundy, working most of his life for him and other patrons of the art-loving ducal family.

Mabuse, with Van Orley (see plate 86), may be called the chief representatives of the Renaissance style in the Netherlands. His natural feeling for volumes and satisfying balance, for elegance and richness in surface and decoration, was increased and developed by his work at the Burgundian court and by his contacts with such princely patrons as Margaret of Austria and Christian of Denmark; Charles V and Eleanor of Portugal sat to him for portraits, for Mabuse excelled also in this kind of painting.

Most of all, however, he profited by a trip to Italy in 1508–09. None of his Northern contemporaries ever achieved a painting of the Madonna and Child that combined so much courtly grace and decoration with the solidity of sculpture. Other painters, seized with an admiration for the monumental Italian style, hardened their human forms into granite blocks, but this picture contrasts shining hair and soft flesh with the angularity and weight of the stone architecture in a way that demonstrates how high a degree of skill Mabuse achieved in the understanding of plastic form.

90 ROBERT CAMPIN (MASTER OF FLÉMALLE; about 1380–1444). Flemish. *St. John the Baptist and Henricus Werl* and *St. Barbara*. Painted 1438. Oil on wood; each panel, 39¾ x 18½"

These two panels are considered among the best of Campin's work and are quite evidently the wings of a triptych whose central panel is lost. The date of 1438 is given in an inscription at the bottom of the left panel, reading: *Ano milleno c q̄ter et octo hic fecit effigie depigi mistre Hiricus Werlis mgr̄ Colon.* In this year Heinrich, or Henricus, von Werl, a Franciscan and a professor at the University of Cologne, was present at the Council at Basle (1431–39). He is shown kneeling, with his hands in an attitude of prayer, but the face, scholarly and worldly, turns toward the spectator. His patron, the bearded St. John, is shown with his attribute, the white lamb. Through the open window a hilly landscape is seen, with buildings in the distance. Above the open window are four leaded panes, and in the center of each a coat of arms.

In the companion panel, within a richly furnished, meticulously painted interior, St. Barbara is seated in comfort with her back to a blazing hearth fire, intently reading from a book held in both hands. The bench on which she is sitting, with its reversible back, also appears in Campin's altarpiece belonging to the Mérode family of Brussels. Through the open window in a distant landscape is a tower under construction—St. Barbara's main attribute. Her expression is one of studious calm, with no sign of disquiet at the thought of her future imprisonment. Other attributes, the signs of her purity, are the iris flower, the water ewer, and the basin with the towel hanging above.

Campin, first known as the Master of the Mérode Altarpiece from the painting mentioned above, was later known as the Master of Flémalle, after an abbey from which three of his paintings are presumed to have come. Hulin de Loo identified him with Robert Campin, and believed that he must have worked at one time under the Van Eycks. From the documents it is known that in 1406, at about the age of 28, Campin settled in Tournai. In 1427 he received two important apprentices, Rogier van der Weyden and Jacques Daret. He is now credited with many paintings and other works of art. Some critics of importance, however, disbelieving the documents and failing to see any of the fundamental contrasts in temperament between the bodies of work adjudged to the two men, simply consider Campin's work to be that of Van der Weyden early in his career.

91 ROGIER VAN DER WEYDEN (1400–64). Flemish. *The Descent from the Cross*. Painted about 1435. Oil on wood, 86⅝ x 103⅛"

Rogier painted this masterwork about 1435 for the chapel of the Confraternity of the Crossbowmen in the Church of Our Lady of Louvain. Charles V's sister, Mary of Hungary, bought it at a very high price and took it with her to Spain in 1556. The document that records its delivery to the Escorial in 1574 alludes to wings showing *The Resurrection* and *The Four Evangelists*, but these have unfortunately been lost.

The first impression made by the ten large plastic figures crowded together against a gold ground is a startling reminder of sculptured Gothic altarpieces. A series of repeated swaying S-curves keeps the entire grandiose composition in an effective balance of tensions and resolutions. The numbing grief of all the mourners is symbolized by the heavy downward movement of the body of Christ, paralleled and underlined by that of the fainting Virgin, which follows the same course.

A contemporary scholar has made a careful study of theological attitudes toward the Passion of Christ and the compassion, or fellow-suffering, of the Virgin Mary. Bernard of Clairvaux had meditated on this dual grief in the twelfth century, and in the fourteenth and fifteenth centuries it became a favorite theme for theologians and artists. In Rogier's paintings, especially, we find a deep concern with the swooning body and the sorrowing face of Mary. Dr. Erwin Panofsky in his recently published *Early Netherlandish Painting* has skillfully summarized the painter's intention in this extraordinary painting by stating that it was focused not "on action nor even 'drama' but on the fundamental problem of compressing a maximum of passion into a form as rigorously disciplined as a Shakespearean sonnet. . . . His youthful and almost sensual vitality were soon to give way to austere unworldliness."

92 ROGIER VAN DER WEYDEN (1400–64). Flemish. *The Virgin and Child*. Painted about 1437. Oil on wood, 39⅜ x 20½″

The theme of the divine Child riffling the pages of an illuminated book held by his Mother appears repeatedly in Flemish paintings. But where Jan van Eyck achieved an effect of casual ease and informality, Rogier, setting the pair like a monumental sculptured group in an architectural niche, made certain that no one would doubt their otherworldliness. It is implicit in every lineament of face, hands, and drapery, proclaiming even without the testimony of the angel, hovering above her and offering a jeweled crown, that the lovely, serious Virgin is indeed the Queen of Heaven.

93 Attributed to DIERIC BOUTS (about 1420–73). Flemish. *The Nativity*. Painted about 1450. Oil on wood, 31½ x 20⅞″

This charming picture (companion piece of *The Visitation* and *The Adoration of the Magi* reproduced on plates 77 and 78), shows the calm Virgin with the three angels adoring the newborn Child and attended by Joseph, while three shepherds peer through windows into the ruined stable. In the Prado the painting is prettily entitled "The Adoration of the Angels." A full generation before, the motif of the tiny Infant lying exposed on the bare ground had been put into the masterly painting in Dijon (the Master of Flémalle). Petrus Christus, working in Bruges, used it again in his quadripartite work in the Museum at Berlin, dated 1452 and thus of about the same period as this *Nativity*, presumably painted in Haarlem. In the foreground of the Prado picture, the splendid angel clad in brocade is a forerunner of a characterful angel which Hugo van der Goes painted about 1476 in his great triptych for the Portinari family—now in the Uffizi at Florence.

94 HANS MEMLING (about 1433–94). Flemish. *The Presentation of the Christ Child in the Temple* (right wing of plate 80). Painted about 1470. Oil on wood, 37⅜ x 24¾″

This painting, the right wing of *The Three Kings Altarpiece* (of which *The Adoration of the Magi*, plate 80, is the center), is the most solemn and austere of the three panels that make up the triptych. Whereas the worship of the Wise Men from the East, and the homage of the little angels in *The Nativity* (plate 81) were honors without precedent accorded to the holy Mother and Child and received with dignity and grace, the Presentation in the Temple was a ritual act, written, according to St. Luke, "in the law of the Lord."

Memling has used a variety of devices to intensify the hush of a holy place; the spacious square glimpsed behind St. Joseph at the left contrasts with the shadowy space within, where, on a little raised pavement, the high priest takes the baby from his Mother's arms. Mary's erect body emphasizes the verticality of all the architectural lines, especially of the lofty, uncompromising columns. The bald, extremely dignified priest steps forward and extends his arms with a measured gesture that expresses his awareness of the solemn act that he performs.

Only St. Luke tells the story of the Presentation in the Temple, and we may assume that the older woman in the white coif is the prophetess Anna who "coming in that instant . . . gave thanks likewise unto the Lord," and spoke of the Child "to all them that looked for redemption in Jerusalem." The robed priest is presumably the "just and devout" Simeon, who on receiving the baby Jesus in his arms uttered the beautiful hymn called the *Nunc Dimittis*: "Lord, now lettest thou thy servant depart in peace, according to thy word, For mine eyes have seen thy salvation" (Luke 2:29–30).

95 JOACHIM PATINIR (about 1480–1524) and QUENTIN MASSYS (1465–1530). Flemish. *The Temptation of Saint Anthony*. Painted about 1520. Signed: *Opus Joachim -at-nier*. Oil on wood, 61 x 68⅛″

The collaboration between two or more artists on the same picture, which became so common in the seventeenth century, had begun much earlier, and this painting is an excellent example of its merits. The Dutch biographer of painters Carel van Mander, writing at the beginning of the seventeenth century, refers to a fine painting of the Virgin by Joos van Cleve, for which a very beautiful landscape by Joachim Patinir provided the background.

The assumption that the Prado picture is one more instance of Patinir's working with another painter is supported by an old inventory of the Escorial, where *The Temptation of St. Anthony* used to be, listing among its treasures a picture with this subject by "Master Quentin and Master Joachim."

This is one of the few signed paintings by Patinir; but even without the signature it would be easy to ascribe to him the deeply receding, characteristic landscape of this panel, with its wide zigzagging river reflecting golden light amid the blue-green foliage. The personality of Quentin Massys, who combined in his style the nervous mannerisms of Antwerp with a dawning awareness of the Italian Renaissance and its monumental repose, is equally well represented by the fashionably dressed temptresses, who are coached in their assault on poor St. Anthony's high resolves by an old procuress, and aided by a small froglike devil pulling at the Saint's coat tail.

96 ALBRECHT DÜRER (1471–1528). German. *Self-Portrait*. Painted 1498. Oil on wood, 20½ x 16⅛″

Albrecht Dürer of Nuremberg was the greatest representative of humanistic culture north of the Alps. His boundless curiosity and deep intelligence, and his frank admiration and emulation of what he found on his two trips to Italy combine with his rare gifts as an artist to make him one of the most notable figures of the northern Renaissance.

After some training from his father, who was a goldsmith, he served an apprenticeship with Michael Wolgemut, the painter and print-maker. Three years later he set out to see the world, traveling for several years through Germany and Switzerland, and in 1494, after a brief visit to his native city, setting out for Venice.

In 1498, a couple of years after his return to Germany, he recorded his appearance at the age of twenty-six, in this stylish and self-conscious self-portrait, which Panofsky has called "perhaps the first independent self-portrait ever produced."

Italian society over a period of many years had permitted an artist to regard himself as a gentleman while Germans and Netherlanders continued to think of him as an artificer and craftsman; and it can hardly be doubted that Dürer's proud estimate of himself here was a direct result of his having seen at first hand the respect accorded to artists in Italy. He chose to dress himself for the occasion in expensive, elegant, and above all becoming clothes, patently proud of his fine curly hair and handsome appearance. There are other self-portraits by Dürer, but none so boldly and directly pointing out his own importance and good looks.

97 ALBRECHT DÜRER (1471–1528). German. *Adam and Eve*. Painted 1507. Oil on wood; each panel, 82½ x 31½″

In 1507, immediately after returning to Nuremberg from his second trip to Venice, Dürer painted this pair of panels, which together symbolize the Fall of Man. A comparison of these paintings with his engraving of the same subject, made only three years earlier, reveals his extraordinary sensitivity to Italian art and the demonstrable way in which his impressions promptly influenced his own work.

243

In the print the figures exhibit a heavy and distinctly German beauty and monumentality. In the Prado panels they are both more slender: Eve steps forward with a mincing, almost coquettish gait, while Adam's open mouth and curly hair bring to mind Venetian sculpture. Eve's gesture is curious, for with her left hand she absent-mindedly accepts the apple offered by the serpent, looking out of the picture with an abstracted gaze that shows no awareness of the solemn portent of her action. With her right hand she touches a branch of the apple tree, from which hangs a label, stating in Latin that the German Albrecht Dürer made the picture 1507 years after the Virgin Birth, and bearing the artist's signature, the monogram, A. D.

These panels were once owned by Queen Christina of Sweden, who gave them to Philip IV. There are variant workshop copies in Florence and in Mainz, with animals added as accompaniments to the first parents.

98 HANS BALDUNG (about 1480–1545). German. *Harmony* or *The Three Graces*. Painted about 1540. Oil on wood, 59½ x 24"

These three semi-nude young women, with their musical instruments and attendant *putti*, cannot simply be dismissed as the Graces, the three who in the words of Spenser, "on men all gracious gifts bestow." Their elaborately dressed hair and jewels, the lute and viol, the books from which they read or sing, and even the naked babies playing with the swan in a harmonious and beautiful setting of leafy oak trees and laurels would be compatible enough with this interpretation. But a serpent may be glimpsed curling around a tree, and there is a companion piece in the Prado which suggests a more solemn meaning; when the two pictures are paired perhaps we have here the image of vain and carefree Youth, as contrasted with Old Age and Death in the companion piece.

It is generally agreed that Hans Baldung (called Grien) painted these enigmatic panels very late in his life, probably about 1540. He was born of a good family in Swabia, and worked for a couple of years in his youth in the studio of Albrecht Dürer. In 1517 he went to Strasbourg, where he remained for the rest of his life. In addition to painting altarpieces, he also designed stained glass. His drawings are of the finest, and his woodcuts impressive and full of invention.

99 JAN VAN SCOREL (1495–1562). Dutch. *Portrait of a Humanist*. Painted 1524–30. Oil on wood, 26⅜ x 20½"

This intelligent, dog-loving man is supposed by Don F. J. Sánchez Cantón to be a student, indeed very probably a writer on the Bible, for the building at which he points has the characteristic architecture of the Tower of Babel as represented by artists of the sixteenth century. If this supposition is correct it may be possible in time to identify the subject.

Jan van Scorel is thought to have been born at the town of Scorel near Alkmaar in North Holland, and to have studied first with Cornelis Buys in the latter city. A second teacher of Scorel was the well-known Amsterdam painter, Jacob Cornelisz. About 1517 Scorel sought out Jan Gossaert in Utrecht and Albrecht Dürer in Nuremberg. Later he visited Venice and accompanied Utrecht members of the Jerusalem Brotherhood on a pilgrimage to the Holy Land. He spent several years in Rome where he was influenced by Raphael, and in Glasgow there is a copy by him of Raphael's *Madonna of the Oak Tree*.

In 1524 at the age of twenty-nine he returned to Utrecht, where he established a large studio or workshop. There he painted many fine portraits, especially rows of half-length portraits of pilgrims in the habit of their brotherhood, painted on horizontal strips. Scorel also painted many religious pictures. In 1528 he was made a canon of the cathedral at Utrecht. His *Portrait of a Humanist* was bought by the Prado in 1935.

100 ALBRECHT DÜRER (1471–1528). German. *Portrait of an Unknown Man*. Painted 1524. Oil on wood, 19⅝ x 14⅛"

In the last decade of his life, his thirst for seeing new things and meeting new people in no way quenched, Dürer and his wife traveled for two years, in 1520 and 1521, in the Low Countries. They stayed several times in Antwerp at an inn kept by one Jobst Planckfelt, whose likeness the painter recorded in a wonderful drawing, dated 1520, now in Frankfurt.

The Prado portrait, which was long and quite erroneously called a portrait of the Nuremberg patrician Hans Imhoff, shows the strongest resemblance to Planckfelt as we know him from the drawing; the mouth and shape of nostrils are the same, but most of all, the eyes in both likenesses are shadowed by a strong fleshy formation, drooping slantwise over the outer corners, which makes the identification with the innkeeper hard to deny. The objection has been made that the man in the Prado picture is clearly learned and highly placed in the world, and could not therefore represent Planckfelt, but this hardly seems valid enough to outweigh the facial resemblance, nor does the argument that the furred garment is too elegant for an innkeeper seem convincing, for innkeepers like other people could be expected to wear their Sunday clothes when sitting for a formal portrait.

Dürer's methodical notebook of his journey records, along with such quaintly delightful bits of information as his wife's receiving of a small green parrot as a gift, the fact that in 1521 he made a careful oil portrait of Planckfelt. All would still be well were the portrait in the Prado not dated; but it is dated, and according to some scholars, the date is 1524. The drawing of the last digit is extremely ambiguous, however, and because of the narrow space it occupies, better read as a 1 than a 4. Thus, there is the strongest probability that we have here a portrait, painted in 1521, of Dürer's Antwerp host, Jobst Planckfelt.

101 MARINUS VAN REYMERSWAELE (about 1495–1567). Dutch. *A Banker and His Wife*. Signed: *Marinus me feci a d 1539*. Oil on wood, 32⅝ x 38⅛"

Paradoxically, this most eccentric and mannered of artists, in choosing to paint a banker and his wife at work on their accounts, harks back to a very old theme. It had been used nearly a century before by Petrus Christus in the so-called *St. Eligius* in the Robert Lehman Collection; nearer to Marinus' own time the theme had been used by Quentin Massys in a fine genre scene, dated 1514, in the Louvre, and it is this picture on which *A Banker and His Wife* is based. The genre scenes that Marinus evolved and developed bear dates from 1521 to 1558. In spite of their strangeness, they must have been extremely popular, for most of his themes are repeated again and again with slight variations.

The date of the painter's birth is not certain, but we know that he was a native of Zeeland in South Holland, and during the first decade of the sixteenth century was apprenticed to a glass painter of Antwerp. He seems to have left Antwerp after he became a free master, and worked mostly in Middleburg on the island of Walcheren.

Marinus' personal kind of Mannerism that renders all his genre pictures so cluttered, tense, and fascinating is a very different thing indeed from the Flemish Mannerism that flourished especially in Antwerp around 1520. That style had been characterized by an overloading of ornament, goldsmith's work, and costume detail, and by a fluttering, pervasive movement that exceeded the demands of the action that was taking place. Marinus was a much more talented artist than most of those Antwerp Mannerists, and his extraordinary interiors, crowded with the still life for which he had such a predilection, are always well composed and balanced, and characterized by a taut kind of drawing which, though bizarre to a degree, is nevertheless beautiful.

102 MARINUS VAN REYMERSWAELE (about 1495–1567). Dutch. *St. Jerome in His Study*. Signed on book rack: *Mdad me fecit A⁰ 1551*. Oil on wood, 29½ x 39¾"

St. Jerome in His Study was one of the subjects most often repeated by this artist, doubtless because the bearded, aged scholar-saint with all his paraphernalia of books, writing materials, and skull offered unlimited opportunities for the expression of the painter's peculiar personality.

When Dürer was in the Netherlands in 1521 he painted a *St. Jerome* for a Portuguese business man of his acquaintance, Rodrigo Fernandez, who was living in Antwerp. This picture, signed and dated 1521, is now in the Lisbon Museum. In Antwerp it had soon become a favorite source for painters of the circle of Quentin Massys, and they repeated the theme with endless variations.

Dürer's paintings made during the journey in the Low Countries were customarily preceded by drawings, and Van Reymerswaele might have known a drawing for the *Jerome,* the painting itself, or one of the Flemish pictures depending on the Lisbon painting. In any case, in this rendition of the theme made thirty years after Dürer's painting, Van Reymerswaele's mannerisms and nervosity have increased almost to the point of madness, but he has stamped his creation with undeniable style and design.

103 ANTHONIS MOR (1519–1576). Dutch. *Joanna of Austria.* Painted about 1560. Oil on canvas, 76¾ x 41″

Doña Juana (or Joanna) of Austria, the daughter of Charles V and Empress Isabella, was born in Madrid in 1535, and was thus fourteen years younger than her half-sister, Margaret of Parma, and eight younger than her brother Philip II. She is said to have had a brilliant mind, and at eight years to have known Latin and played well various musical instruments. Just under the age of seventeen in 1552 she was married to Juan, the eldest son of the King of Portugal. Two years after the marriage Juan died, and eighteen days later Joanna bore a son. He was named Sebastian, and at the age of twenty-four, as King of Portugal, got himself killed in a foolhardy expedition against the Moors in Morocco.

At a time when Joanna was not long a widow and Philip had gone a-marrying to England, Charles V, deciding to use the talents of his daughter and perhaps also to divert her from thinking over-much about her bereavement, appointed her Governess of Castile, which she ruled from Valladolid.

The personal life she chose to lead there was severely simple. Her clear intelligence was valuable in perceiving the needs of her territories, and her firm will in applying remedies. Her defense of the Church against heresy was unfaltering and severe, culminating in a wholesale auto-da-fé on May 21, 1559. It must have been soon after that event, perhaps early in 1560, that Joanna's portrait was painted by Anthonis Mor. The painter had been brought to Spain at that time by Philip II, when that King returned from England with affairs to engage him en route in the Netherlands.

Anthonis Mor, the artist who painted this portrait of Juana and of others of the Court, was called also Mor van Dashorst, from the name of his family estate. He was active internationally and was known in Italy and in Spain as Antonio Moro, and in England as Sir Anthony More. Born in or near Utrecht, he studied there under Jan van Scorel. In 1547 he was admitted to the painters' guild in Antwerp, and two years later in Brussels became official painter to the powerful Cardinal Antoine Granvelle, later minister to Margaret of Parma, Regent of the Netherlands.

Mor was twice in Spain and Portugal. His painting is perhaps somewhat tight in handling and subdued in color, yet it is superbly right in drawing and strong in modeling. His portraits, whether of nobles or of their dwarfs, show deep insight and respect for personality, thus forecasting the art of Velázquez.

104 ANTHONIS MOR (1519–1576). Dutch. *Mary Tudor of England.* Signed below the ruffle of the sleeve: *Antonius Mor pingebat 1554.* Oil on wood, 42⅞ x 33½″

Anthonis Mor is represented in the Prado by no less than fifteen portraits. This one, which belonged to Charles V, represents the unfortunate Queen of England, who for the last four years of her frustrated life was the neglected wife of Charles' son, Philip II.

Mary had been born at Greenwich in 1516, the daughter of Henry VIII and Catherine of Aragon. Although she was intellectually precocious and endowed with brilliant gifts, during most of her youth she suffered such indignities at the hands of her father, and also after his death at the hands of her brother, Edward VI, that her acrid and mean appearance could almost be excused. She did not come to the throne until 1553 when she was thirty-seven, and it was in the following year that she was finally married to Philip II, a marriage intimately bound up with her passionate wish to nullify her father's Protestantism and to re-establish the Catholic faith in England.

It was in the year when her marriage was under immediate consideration that Mor painted her portrait, and it gives evidence that this sound portraitist was more devoted to truth than charity. Mor has painted her holding in her hand the red Tudor rose, her person bedecked with a fortune in jewels. Her dress is of gray cut velvet with a purple velvet coat. Charles V, when he retired to the monastery of Yuste in 1556 to spend there his last two years of life, took with him this portrait of his daughter-in-law, for he was proud of having arranged this apparent alliance between England and Spain.

A good replica of the portrait belongs to the Isabella Stewart Gardner Museum in Boston.

105 JAN BRUEGHEL (1568-1625) and HENDRICK DE CLERCK (1570–1630). Flemish. *Abundance and the Four Elements.* Painted 1600–10. Oil on copper, 20⅛ x 25¼″

Jan, called "Velvet," Brueghel was a member of the large family of painters that descended from the incomparable Pieter Bruegel the Elder, painter and print maker. In the Prado alone there are more than forty paintings, all or in part by him. At the end of the fifteenth century painters often specialized in one kind of painting, becoming especially skillful in depicting figures, or animals, or landscapes, or still life. Thus the practice of collaboration developed, and we find Brueghel, as here, supplying the landscape and fauna in a picture where the figures were painted by another artist.

Hendrick de Clerck, a Brussels painter, worked in two somewhat dissimilar styles; his traditional large-scale figures were reserved for conventional religious paintings, of which he seems to have made a great many. On the other hand he perfected a small-figured and delicate, decorative manner of painting which he employed in sprightly mythological and mundane subjects.

His very ably constructed and charming little figures in this picture represent the Four Elements disposed in a luxuriantly verdant landscape, in happy attendance on the Goddess of Abundance in the center. In her arm she holds a cornucopia filled with fruit, on her head she wears ripe grain, and above her hover a pair of exuberant *putti* with a wreath of flowers. The happy Earth reclines at the right with tulips and grapes in her hands. Air and Fire float at the upper left, Air holding a bird perched on his finger and surrounded by flocks of winged creatures. Fire is typified by a formidable male, flourishing a lighted torch in one hand and an uncomfortably smoking live coal in the other. The dainty personification of Water is seen at the left leaning against a shell and surrounded by fish and crustaceans.

In the early seventeenth century, when this picture was painted, allegorical representations in series, such as the Five Senses, the Four Elements, or the Four Continents, were especially popular.

106 HIERONYMUS BOSCH (about 1450–1516). Dutch. *The Garden of Delights.* Painted about 1500. Oil on wood: central panel, 86⅝ x 76¾″; wings, 86⅝ x 38⅛″

Surely Bosch's most ambitious painting was this *Garden of Delights,* with the action of its three panels set in marvelous landscapes of a sort never seen by man, populated with probably a thousand charmingly drawn and accurately painted figures of human beings and of creatures even stranger. One of the early titles of the triptych was *The Strawberry Tree (El Madroño).* José de Sigüenza, writing in 1600–05, called it "the picture of the vain glory and brief enjoyment of the strawberry, or *madroño,* of which the fragrance is no sooner sensed than it is gone." The strawberry tree exists in nature, and indeed is found with a bear beneath it on the coat of arms of the city of Madrid.

A more persuasive interpretation of this masterpiece than that of Sigüenza, and perhaps somewhat overdrawn, is that of Wilhelm Fränger. In *The Millennium of Hieronymus Bosch* (University of Chicago Press, 1951), he points out that the subject matter of the triptych is such that it could hardly have been commissioned by an orthodox Christian foundation, nor yet by an orthodox Christian layman. It could only have been made, he believes, for one of the cultist groups such as the Adamites, or the Brethren and Sisters of the Free Spirit, both of which heretical sects flourished in Bosch's day. These worshiped God in a direct, unorthodox, and somewhat pantheistic way, believing that those who had reached "complete absorption in God" had no need for prayer or sacraments; they also held that the satisfaction of sensual desire was to be commended and would not "stain the soul." The Adamites, as the name of their cult suggests, especially venerated the male parent of mankind who, before the Fall, lived simply, walked with God, and was naked and unashamed. Evidently it was a nudist cult.

Bosch's triptych bears on the closed wings a wondrous picture of the third day of Creation—the establishment of the vegetable kingdom. On the interior of the left wing, it may be noted that in painting the Garden of Eden the artist has chosen the one scene from the story which would most concern the Adamites—namely, the marriage of the first man with the first woman.

In the central panel the marvelous eventfulness makes it impossible to comment in detail. Considering that the meadows are swarming with attractive young men and delightful young women, in pairs, it is a striking circumstance that no children are to be seen. The cult must have been regulated as strictly as the band of Diana's nymphs. Here and there, as the early title of the work suggests, monster strawberries are being gnawed at with evident relish. In this enchanted garden no color line is drawn, and the negresses help the artist by the linear verve of their raven-black figures.

The right wing, lit by murky fires, represents the Inferno, and is as full of surprising details as the other panels. Not the least of these is the nearby pig which attempts to seduce an unwilling man. She wears the coif of the Beguines, another liberal sect, and one that was evidently unloved by our Adamites (or Brethren and Sisters of the Free Spirit), the curious cult which presumably sponsored this beguiling picture of an earthly paradise.

107 HIERONYMUS BOSCH (about 1450–1516). Dutch. *The Garden of Delights* (detail of plate 106)

In the left shutter of his triptych, depicting the Garden of Eden, Bosch omits the usual subjects: the Creation of Eve, the Temptation, and the Expulsion, in order to stress—almost to discover—the Marriage of Adam and Eve as an event of especial solemnity. In the words of Dr. Fränger, whose interpretation of the triptych has been mentioned in the preceding commentary, "They both remain enclosed in the magnetic field of their Creator's transcendence . . . as He bestows on them the sacrament of marriage." The Book of Genesis tells how the Lord God brought Eve to Adam, and how Adam proclaimed her bone of his bone and flesh of his flesh. The trancelike mood of the painting emphasizes the significance of this first marriage. The strangely formed Tree of Knowledge behind Adam was copied from an engraving of *The Flight into Egypt* by the German artist Schongauer.

108 HIERONYMUS BOSCH (about 1450–1516). Dutch. *The Garden of Delights* (detail of plate 106)

Any part of the panel chosen at random is filled with delightful incidents. The portion illustrated here is from the lower left corner of the main panel. Nobody could be happier than the young couples, one safely inside a soap bubble and the other looking from the

window in a pomegranate. Yet all is not pleasure, even here. What does the black rat portend, approaching the encased man through the glass cylinder? And, in the lower right corner, the red berry which the platypus is feeding to the sick man in the blue tube—is it curative or lethal? A magnified finch farther up is giving a purple berry to a poor fellow who is turning the color of death, and a wildly anxious youth nearby is trying to save his girl from a similar fate. Apparently age and illness do occur in this Paradise, but at least the way out is clear and easy. In the center of the scene is a figure, inverted and in the act of drowning, a man, according to Dr. Fränger, who is committing suicide because he has failed to rid himself of the feeling of shame at his nudity.

109 HIERONYMUS BOSCH (about 1450–1516). Dutch. *The Garden of Delights* (detail of plate 106)

More fantastic episodes are seen in this section from the lower right of Bosch's endlessly fascinating central panel. At the top is a gallant man bringing a monster strawberry to his lady friend; in the lower corner diagonally opposite are three men enjoying their fruits with no thought of sharing. On the grassy bank near the owl lies an earnest and charming maiden beside a man whose head is enclosed in a blue capsule. He is, or so we are told by Dr. Fränger, a "twenty-third-degree" or adept member of the sect, engaged in the instruction of a newcomer. In the lower right corner, a still more experienced leader is teaching the tenets of the group to another, not-too-promising-looking female who is protected by a glass cylinder. Readers who find themselves puzzled are referred to Dr. Fränger's book, but should bear in mind that this Garden is primarily for Delights rather than for Learning.

110 HIERONYMUS BOSCH (about 1450–1516). Dutch. *The Garden of Delights* (detail of plate 106)

Hieronymus Bosch was especially famous in his own day for his paintings of Hell, such as the one on the right wing of *The Garden of Delights,* of which this is a detail. Even nocturnal views of our own modern steel centers such as Gary and Pittsburgh pale before the awfulness of Bosch's Infernos, for besides the lurid flames and smoke issuing from unexpected orifices, Bosch thickly populates his dreadful region with countless monstrously formed creatures, some of them suffering hideously, others inflicting on their fellows deeds of ingenious cruelty with insensate *sang-froid.* And what of the pair of gigantic skewered human ears with a knife blade between for mowing down the terrified people? Most arresting amidst all this unreasoning violence is the calm and reasonable regard of a pair of earnest eyes set in an intelligent face with wide, sensitive mouth firmly shut, yet humane, and indicative of a rich personality.

There can be little doubt that this is Bosch's own portrait, for it resembles in its essential features an extant portrait drawing of him at a more advanced age. The wide difference in his apparent age in the two portraits may mean that *The Garden of Delights* was painted as early as 1485, the date proposed by the German critic, Dr. Baldass.

111 HIERONYMUS BOSCH (about 1450–1516). Dutch. *The Temptation of St. Anthony.* Painted about 1510–12. Oil on wood, 27½ x 20″

According to José de Sigüenza, writing about the year 1600, the devout and contemplative soul, such as that of St. Anthony, may be assisted by divine grace, in which event the things the Enemy presents to his outer and inner eye will not cause him anger or other irregular passions, nor move him from his purpose.

In this little panel, the good St. Anthony seems so untroubled and pensive that it might better have been entitled a *Meditation* than a *Temptation.* The Saint sits intimately with nature and appears to have reached a happy condition where the demons are small and even rather well disposed toward him. The companionable pig lying nearby is his familiar attribute. It is usually black, and in making it light, Bosch probably intended to convey more strongly than any previous artist the idea that the good hermit had cleansed its porcine nature of all sensuality.

112 HIERONYMUS BOSCH (about 1450–1516). Dutch. *The Adoration of the Magi.* Painted about 1500. Signed lower left of main panel: *Iheronimus bosch.* Oil on wood: central panel, 54⅜ x 28⅜″; wings, 54⅜ x 13″

This finely proportioned and minutely finished triptych, with wings only thirteen inches wide, yet providing lovely landscapes with buildings and expressive figures, is more conventional than most of the works by Bosch. It is considered by the German authority on Netherlandish painting, Max J. Friedländer, to be the artist's masterpiece.

In the main panel the traditional ruined stable, where the newborn Child has been laid in the manger, is alive with peeping shepherds and also with odd-looking people who stand just within the stable door. Near the horizon loom the fantastic buildings of a town—perhaps Bethlehem, perhaps the dream city of the celestial New Jerusalem. Somewhat nearer are two mounted armies approaching one another, and here too critics have a choice—whether these are the friendly escorts of two of the Kings, or whether on the contrary they typify the violence and evil of all the world, which lying outside the stable yard, is thus not sanctified and protected by the presence of the Holy Family.

In the left wing of the triptych kneels the donor, sponsored by St. Peter, while at a little distance sits St. Joseph, protected by the walls of a ruined castle while he dries

246

diapers before a bonfire. As in the main panel, evil is rampant beyond the charmed enclosure as peasant couples sinfully dance to a bagpiper's tune. The right wing shows the donor's gentle wife accompanied by St. Agnes. The Saint's familiar lamb lies calm and safe within the blessed precinct, but beyond in the meadow a peasant has been brought down by a ravening wolf, and his wife is pursued by another.

113 HIERONYMUS BOSCH (about 1450–1516). Dutch. *The Adoration of the Magi* (detail of plate 112)

Bosch shows here the traditional Three Kings, or Magi, from the East, come to worship the newborn Christ Child. The negro King is an especially handsome figure. Peering at the holy event from within the stable are some mysterious men, usually supposed to be attendants from the Kings' retinues. The Prado's fine earlier painting of the Epiphany by Memling (plate 80) shows a similar group, including a bearded and turbaned Oriental who could be a high-strung camel driver. In Bosch's picture, it is no surprise to find that this mildly overwrought individual has become pronouncedly leering and crazy, for Bosch loved demons and queer human beings. If one is to believe Lotte Brand Philip's article in the *Art Bulletin* (December, 1953)—and the weight of her evidence from medieval Jewish speculative writings is not easy to resist—this queer, helmeted, seminude man may be the Antichrist himself. Dr. Philip finds passages from obscure late medieval writings that argue in favor of the theory that the Three Kings themselves alternated between good and evil tendencies. Bosch, it is claimed, was sufficiently curious about the literature of diabolism and distortion of the human mind to have given visual form in this triptych to elaborate speculations of the kind cited.

114 HIERONYMUS BOSCH (about 1450–1516). Dutch. *The Hay Wagon* (central panel). Painted about 1485. Signed: *Iheronimus bosch.* Oil on wood, 53⅛ x 39⅜″

The wings of this triptych represent, as do many of the shutters painted by Bosch, *The Earthly Paradise* at the left and *The Inferno* at the right. Only the central part of the triptych is reproduced here. The theme follows an old Flemish proverb: "The world is a haystack; each plucks from it as much as he can get." All sorts of people are involved in the plucking. A tonsured monk is between the wheels, and following on horseback are a pope, a bishop, a king, a duke, and others. The only people immune from the scramble are the lovers making music atop the load of hay.

High in the sky is Christ watching with arms outspread as though in grief. In the foreground of the picture are illustrated the seven deadly sins, Pride (about to fall),

Envy, Wrath (above the rest—the violent fellow stabbing his victim in the throat), Sloth, Lust (the woman listening to the sinful music of the piper), Avarice, and Gluttony.

115 HIERONYMUS BOSCH (about 1450–1516). Dutch. *The Garden of Delights* (detail of plate 106)

A strip across the upper part of the central panel gives an informative aspect of this very human earthly paradise. The nature of the lower half of the picture has been revealed by the details shown in plates 108 and 109, where the abundance of happy couples can be seen in all sorts of situations. The wide upper half of the panel, partly devoted to astonishing vegetative growth, is in the main a zone revealing the important business of mating the unmatched young maidens and bachelors. The maidens are located in a circular wading pool. Some balance apples on their heads, others carry storks, both probably having the same significance. But what of those crows? In any case the pool is encircled with something which holds the wistful attention of the girls: it is a ring of young male riders, some mounted on pretty horses, others on griffons, camels, pigs, or unicorns, and many performing acrobatic feats, the better to ensnare mates for themselves. One girl is climbing out of the pool in pursuit.

116 PIETER BRUEGEL, the Elder (about 1525–69). Flemish. *The Triumph of Death* (detail of plate 117)

Pieter Bruegel the Elder, many of whose descendants were also painters, remains far and away the most gifted member of his family. He is thought to have been born in the little town of Bruegel, from which he takes his name, near Breda in North Brabant. The later generations of the family spelled the name with an *h* (Brueghel). Jan Brueghel, who with Hendrick de Clerck, painted *The Abundance and Four Elements* (plate 105), was a younger son of Pieter the Elder. The village of Bruegel is not many miles from 's-Hertogenbosch, where Hieronymus Bosch died a few years before, in 1516; and much of Bruegel's early work, especially his drawings for engravers, reveal in their fantasy and satire Bosch's strong influence.

Bruegel went to Antwerp perhaps as early as 1540 and became the apprentice there of Pieter Coeck van Aelst. He was made a free master in Antwerp in 1551. In 1563 he moved to Brussels and married Maria, Pieter Coeck's daughter, whom he had watched growing up almost from her infancy. Bruegel made a trip to Italy in 1552–53, but the experience left little mark on his essentially northern style.

According to Van Mander, the early chronicler of Dutch and Flemish painters, it was Bruegel's practice to dress in a peasant's disguise to attend country weddings and carnivals where he could make the careful studies of types that so enrich his works. He pos-

sessed a great power of welding innumerable truthfully observed details into organized commentaries on life and its vanities. As he grew older he simplified his compositions, using fewer figures and disciplining their arrangement.

The detail from *The Triumph of Death* reproduced here is the landscape in which Death accomplishes his gruesome victory, a suitable landscape—all waste, parched country with no living vegetation, ships burning on the distant sea, towns afire along the coast, and rotting human bodies hanging on scaffolds or exposed on gibbets. See the following commentary for an account of this painting.

117 PIETER BRUEGEL, the Elder (about 1525–69). Flemish. *The Triumph of Death.* Painted 1560–62. Tempera and oil on wood, 46⅛ x 63¾″

The ultimate triumph of death over life was a favorite subject of the late Middle Ages and one taken readily to the hearts of people who had been shaken and chastened by repeated outbreaks of the plague that decimated whole cities and provinces. Two famous Italian treatments of this subject were the decorations in the Palazzo Sclafani at Palermo, and the frescoes by Francesco Traini in the Camposanto at Pisa, lamentably damaged in the bombings of World War II. Triumphs and Dances of Death were very popular in Germany in the sixteenth century, with Dürer, Holbein, and Hans Baldung among the artists who painted these subjects.

Here in Bruegel's grisly treatment Death is a skeleton with a scythe, riding a scrawny horse whose cinnamon-colored hide scarcely covers his protruding bones. But he has many skeletal helpers, violently dragging the living to their deaths, or methodically carting off hundreds of skulls. The numberless figures and episodes scattered rampant on the broad panel make it certain that the picture was painted no later than 1560 or 1562, before Bruegel had begun to select and simplify.

118 PIETER BRUEGEL, the Elder (about 1525–69). Flemish. *The Triumph of Death* (detail of plate 117)

In the lower left corner of the picture a king, with the royal insignia of crown, scepter, and ermine, and wearing the order of the Golden Fleece about his neck, is overthrown by Death, who exhibits his empty hourglass and rests a hand with mock solicitude on his victim's shoulder. This emphasis on the *transit gloria mundi* recalls Hieronymus Bosch's memorable and moving painting *The Death of the Miser,* now in the National Gallery at Washington. Bruegel insists further on the allegory by showing another death-figure in the act of helping himself to the king's gold pieces. Still another sits on a wagon load of skulls and callously amuses himself by playing a hurdy-gurdy, while nearby several worthy women have been interrupted in their spinning by the ultimate disaster.

247

119 PIETER BRUEGEL, the Elder (about 1525–69). Flemish. *The Triumph of Death* (detail of plate 117)

The two happy lovers making music in the lower right corner are unconscious of the grim events taking place around them. Their blissful heedlessness once more recalls Bosch, who had put just such a happy pair atop his Hay Wagon (see plate 114). Near the lovers, several gallants who have been feasting with their lady friends and have suddenly realized the approach of danger are bravely brandishing their futile swords. Stools, a gaming table, cards, and a wine cooler have been ruthlessly upset in the great upheaval.

120 PETER PAUL RUBENS (1577– 1640). Flemish. *Marie de Médicis.* Painted 1622–25. Oil on canvas, 51¼ x 42½"

This splendid portrait, like most of the other paintings that form the Prado's rich collection of works by Rubens, was acquired by Philip IV at the sale of Rubens' effects held after the artist's death in Antwerp.

Marie de Médicis, the French Queen Mother, was the daughter of Francesco de' Medici, Grand Duke of Tuscany. At the time when she sat to Rubens for this likeness, she was approaching the age of fifty and had been a widow for more than twelve years, since the death of Henri IV in 1610. In spite of her widow's headdress and her richly somber costume of black and white, her double chin and heavy jowls, she retains traces of the blond opulence that characterizes all the figures of her in the great allegorical series of scenes from her life, on which Rubens was employed at this same time. This famous cycle, which he designed and executed for her newly constructed Luxembourg Palace, now forms the Medici Gallery of the Louvre.

After its completion she ordered Rubens to prepare a new series devoted to Henri IV, and from 1628–31 Rubens worked on the project. But then the scheme had to be abandoned; it had been slowed down by changes in the architectural plan of the palace and by the intrigue of Marie's advisor Cardinal Richelieu, and most of all by the Queen Mother's quarrel with her son Louis XIII and her resulting financial ruin and banishment. On one sad occasion Rubens actually lent her money. She died in Cologne in 1642.

121 PETER PAUL RUBENS (1577– 1640). Flemish. *The Fall of Man.* Painted 1628–29. Oil on canvas, 93¼ x 72½"

When in 1628–29 Rubens visited Spain for the second time, he made this full-sized copy of Titian's picture, *The Fall of Man* (plate 153). The Titian had been painted about sixty years earlier and was among the works of that artist bought by Philip II; in 1600 it was hanging in the Alcázar at Madrid,

where later it was badly damaged by the dreadful fire in the eighteenth century. Over and beyond the contrast between two great artists, the pictures reveal a complete change in mode of thought and feeling, the Titian typifying the High Renaissance, and the Rubens the Baroque period after the Council of Trent.

As one would expect from a man of Rubens' prodigious ability and strong personality, he did not submit to the restraint which an exact reproduction would have entailed. Little is omitted or introduced, but the figures are softer and more opulent, the color richer, the foliage more actively in motion. Rubens retains Titian's little-boy head for the serpent of temptation, but makes its expression more maliciously puckish.

His most striking change is in the posture of Adam. Titian had pictured him recoiling as though genuinely shocked by Eve's action, whereas Rubens shows him leaning toward her with an expression of incredulous fascination. This gives our Baroque copyist an opportunity to correct what must have seemed to him a fundamental flaw in the Renaissance composition. If he had himself originated it, he would have balanced Eve's determined and beautiful inclination toward the left by Adam's bodily and psychological thrust, accurately calculated, in the opposite direction. And this "correction" he did indeed embody in his copy. When Rubens left Spain he took the canvas back to Antwerp with him, and it was not until after his death that Philip IV was able to acquire it.

122 PETER PAUL RUBENS (1577– 1640). Flemish. *The Garden of Love.* Painted about 1638. Oil on canvas, 78 x 111⅜"

This alluring idyl of youth, beauty, and romance might be regarded as one of Rubens' many tributes to the happiness and fulfillment he found in his marriage to the young and very lovely Hélène Fourment. He had married her in 1630, when she was sixteen, and he was a widower of fifty-three. The decade between his second wedding and his death in 1640 was the most richly productive of his entire career.

The scene is laid in a garden which some have believed to be that of Rubens' house at Antwerp, and the amorous revels are fittingly presided over by a sculptured figure of Venus crouching on a dolphin, and a flock of winged *putti* equipped with all the symbols of love—flowers and turtle doves, a flaming torch, and of course the bow and arrow. The Three Graces ornament a fountain in the center background under the portico. Four women in the center listen to a musician, who strums a lute, but softly, and only as an obbligato to the sweet words that cavaliers are whispering to their loves.

The man at the left wearing the large black hat is possibly an idealized self-portrait, and the lady whom he is persuading, with the assistance of a sympathetic cupid, to join the dance, must be his fair Hélène. She had seven elder sisters, all married, and it has been supposed that Rubens included portraits of various members of the family in the picture. Certain it is, however, that at least two

other figures besides the one with whom he dances have the features of his bride.

It was Rubens' paintings of this type which had such a profound influence on the French painting of the eighteenth century. Watteau developed from it his endless and poetically charming variations on the theme of well-bred young couples held in the suspense of restrained love—his *fêtes galantes*, his *fêtes champêtres*, and his two famous paintings of *The Embarkation for the Island of Cythera*—which never lose their poetic urgency.

123 PETER PAUL RUBENS (1577– 1640). Flemish. *Diana and Callisto.* Painted between 1638–40. Oil on canvas, 79½ x 127⅛"

Poor Callisto! As one of Diana's nymphs she was sworn to virginity. But Jove caught her, bashful and beautiful, and now her condition has begun to evidence itself. Our painting shows at the left a tree over a branch of which is hung a dead deer and beneath which is Diana, whom a negress is bathing. Six disapproving nymphs are undressing the embarrassed and chagrined Callisto. Inexorable Diana will expel her from the group and change her into a bear. Ovid's account in the *Metamorphoses* tells how she fearfully roams the forests, frightened even by the sight of other bears, for she fails to remember that she is now a bear herself.

The landscape for this important work is thought by specialists to have been painted for Rubens by Lucas van Uden. In 1666 the painting was at the Alcázar in the "Gallery of the North Wind." Relegated to the Academy of San Fernando, presumably by Charles III, as exhibiting sinful nudity, it came to the Prado in 1827, but at that time only to the Galleria Riservada, since Ferdinand VII, another prude, did not die until 1833.

124 PETER PAUL RUBENS (1577– 1640). Flemish. *Cephalus and Procris.* Painted about 1637. Oil on wood, 11⅜ x 12⅝"

This is one of the many small oil sketches that Rubens made as a basis for the grand series of large pictures with mythological subjects that Philip IV commissioned him to paint for the hunting lodge, the Torre de la Parada. In some instances he himself painted the large work as well as the sketch; in others, one or another of his assistants painted the big picture, basing it on Rubens' model.

The finished version of *Cephalus and Procris,* based on this sketch by Rubens, was painted on a canvas over six times as large and signed by the little known Peeter Symons of Antwerp. It and many of the other decorations for the Torre de la Parada, by Rubens and his assistants, are now in the Prado. Ten of Rubens' sketches for the Torre are there too, and others are in Brussels, Bayonne, and elsewhere.

The sad story of Cephalus and Procris is related by Ovid in the *Metamorphoses.* Cephalus was a young huntsman, wed hap-

248

pily and faithfully to Procris, but like many mortals, he was loved by a goddess, in this case Aurora. Once when he was overheated from hunting, he craved a breeze and called aloud for Aura the spirit of the wind. His young and suspicious wife thought he was calling on Aurora, and as she sobbed among the bushes, hidden from Cephalus' sight, he mistook the rustling for that of a deer and with his javelin caught her fatally in the throat.

The best-known rendering of the tale is the enchanting picture by Piero di Cosimo in the National Gallery in London, where the black dog mourns opposite the tragic pair after Procris has died of her wound. In Rubens' sketch, Procris is still alive, but seated in an unhappy mood concealed in the bushes near Cephalus, who, weary from the chase, has thrown himself on the ground. He still grasps his javelin and is unaware of his wife's presence, though turning toward the spot where she sits hidden.

125 PETER PAUL RUBENS (1577–1640). Flemish. *Diana's Nymphs Surprised by Satyrs.* Painted 1638–40. Oil on canvas, 50⅜ x 123⅝"

This canvas is admirably shaped for the wild progression of the figures across the scene. Of the seven lovely nymphs, none displays the crescent moon of Diana, but the fierce huntress at the far right, on the point of hurling her javelin, reveals the stern leadership proper to that great goddess of the moon and the chase. The wild goat-legged men have launched their attack with such élan that only the one nymph has had time to seize a weapon, and one in the foreground is still asleep.

The lively harmony of the action and the delightfully fresh color of the entire picture make it one of Rubens' most enjoyable as well as one of his greatest.

Critics all, according to the Prado catalogue, date it 1638–40. According to Max Rooses, Jan Wildens painted the landscape and animals.

126 PETER PAUL RUBENS (1577–1640). Flemish. *St. George Killing the Dragon.* Painted 1607–08. Oil on canvas, 119⅝ x 100¾"

The large canvas, almost ten feet high, is crowded with the excitement of the forms. St. George, with operatic plumed helmet, his cape flying up behind him, has already speared the dragon through the mouth and now raises his sword for the death blow. His splendid dappled gray horse rears over the writhing body of the great lizard whose tail lashes several yards away. The horse with his excited rearing and his luxuriant mane and tail is the hero of this curious composition which recalls Byzantine renditions of the subject.

It is a momentary action, permanently enclosed, for the giant animal could not come down to earth within the confines of the picture frame. Only the lovely princess is placid,

as she waits at the side, holding one of the many sheep that had been sacrificed to the bottomless appetite of the dragon. This eloquent dramatic Baroque of Rubens' early period contrasts sharply with the harsh naturalism of Caravaggio and bears no close resemblance to Annibale Carracci, whose works the young Fleming must have seen in Italy.

Although St. George is one of the most widely venerated saints, the patron of England and of arms and chivalry, the story of his life is veiled in a good deal of cloudy legend. His cult may be traced back to the early centuries of the Christian era at Lydda in Palestine, where his tomb is said to have been discovered. He was a staff officer in Diocletian's army, tortured and martyred because he objected to the Emperor's persecution of the Christians. The story of how he killed a dragon and rescued a king's daughter, as related in *The Golden Legend,* was unknown before the twelfth century.

127 PETER PAUL RUBENS (1577–1640). Flemish. *The Triumph of the Church and the Eucharist.* Painted 1625–28. Oil on wood, 33⅞ x 35⅞"

The Church, typified by a handsome woman, rides in a splendid chariot. She holds before her a monstrance containing the Host and receives a papal tiara from an angel. At the front of the car, the dove of the Holy Ghost perches on an angel's wrist, and a heroic figure on one of the horses carries St. Peter's keys and the pontifical canopy. The bound captives beside the car are Blindness and Ignorance. Beneath the wheels, according to Sánchez Cantón's catalogue, are Anger, Discord, and Hatred; however, a different interpretation by Manuel Trens, in a recent book on the Eucharist in Spanish art, identifies the conspicuous figure under the wheels as Heresy. In the center foreground the globe of the world is seen, encircled by a serpent.

The ponderous architectural frame is the sort that Rubens used in designs for tapestries. This painting was in fact prepared as one of a set of seventeen tapestry designs which the Archduchess Isabella Clara Eugenia, the daughter of Philip II, and Regent of the Netherlands, commissioned from Rubens.

Rubens completed the panels in 1628, receiving 30,000 florins for them. Guided by these small paintings, workers in Rubens' shop made the full-size cartoons from which the weavers in the Brussels factory made their tapestries. The hangings were destined for the Convent of the Descalzas Reales in Madrid. The cartoons remained for a century and a half in one of Madrid's churches, but were scattered at the time of the Napoleonic invasion.

The set of panels painted by Rubens, to which the Prado's *Triumph* belongs, was given to the Royal Collections by a subject of Charles II. Eight are now in the Prado, and the others in former royal palaces. Preparatory drawings and more summary sketches of the series are in the Fitzwilliam Museum at Cambridge, England.

128 PETER PAUL RUBENS (1577–1640). Flemish. *Italian Peasants Dancing.* Painted 1636–40. Oil on wood, 28¾ x 41¾"

In the sale of Rubens' estate, where Philip IV bought it, this comparatively small painting on wood was given the above title. The building in the background with its gently sloped roof and its porch shaded by vines, resting on heavy square supports, is a typical Italian farmhouse, although two shallow *loggie* at the nearer side perhaps seem more Netherlandish. The peasants in any case look Flemish, the men with moplike hair and the women blond and buxom.

A good deal has been said about the dependence of this painting upon old Pieter Bruegel, but the comparison only serves to emphasize the essential difference; Bruegel was always fascinated by the boorishness of his peasants, whereas Rubens seldom could forget the elegance of Flemish aristocracy and the bodily perfection of ancient deities.

Far-fetched it may seem also to compare this vigorous *rond* by Rubens with the familiar *Snap the Whip* by Winslow Homer, yet there is similarity in the contrasting movement of figure groups, which with Rubens serves to emphasize again his marvelous balance or resolution of forces, his rhythmic figure composition, and the glorious drawing and modeling of the bodies. Painted in the last years of his life, the picture is one more example of the extraordinary power and intensity that increased up to the very end.

129 PETER PAUL RUBENS (1577–1640). Flemish. *The Three Graces.* Painted 1639–40. Oil on wood, 87 x 71¼"

This was one of the very last pictures that Rubens painted, and the impact made by these three nudes contrasts markedly with the shadowy formlessness that characterizes the last style of many other artists. The figures are life-size, but much more than life-size in their amplitude.

The Graces, daughters of Jove and the sea-nymph Eurynome, were goddesses of joy and all social occasions, and the garlands of flowers above their heads in the painting recall the fact that these happy creatures are devoted attendants of Venus.

Hélène Fourment, who was about twenty-five when Rubens was painting this picture, served as model for the figure at the left. In the Piccolomini Library at Siena there is a classical sculpture of the Three Graces, a trio of slim girlish figures from which there emanates a cool chasity that set the tone for Raphael and other Renaissance artists who took up the theme.

Rubens' Graces, on the other hand, are redolent of a lush and generous maturity, so frankly stated that the picture was relegated in the late eighteenth century to the private galleries of the Academy of San Fernando, along with other paintings of nudes that the taste of the period branded as indecent.

249

130 JACOB JORDAENS (1593–1678). Flemish. *The Artist's Family in a Garden.* Painted about 1624. Oil on canvas, 71¼ x 73⅝″

Jacob Jordaens deserves a place after Rubens and Van Dyck as the third most important Flemish painter of the seventeeth century. In fact his robustly wholesome, lusty paintings, executed in a style perfectly adapted to their subject matter, constitute a wholly original aspect of the art of their time and place, roughly comparable to that of Steen in Dutch painting. Jordaens had only one master that we know of, an artist who had also taught Rubens—the painter Adam van Noort. His daughter Catharina became Jordaens' wife in 1616, just about the time that the young painter was admitted to the Guild of St. Luke as a water colorist. But with the tutelage of Van Noort alone Jordaens would never have developed into the strong artist that he became. Though he never worked in the studio of Rubens, directly under this greatest painter of the time, he was enormously influenced throughout his life by the example of Rubens and his art.

Jordaens painted himself several times in family groups that make no aristocratic pretentions, but are frankly and comfortably bourgeois and solvent. Here he stands at the right, holding his lute, and looking remarkably like an engraved portrait of himself that Pieter de Jode made after a lost Van Dyck. Opposite him is an attractive young servant holding a basket of fruit; she stands beside Jordaens' wife, who is well dressed in a large ruff and wearing lace cuffs, and is seated in a chair placed in the garden beneath a sculptured group. His little daughter Isabella, who leans against her mother's knee, was born in June of 1617, and since she looks about six, the picture was probably painted around 1624. In an earlier work in the gallery at Cassel, Jordaens had painted himself playing the lute in a group composed of members of the Van Noort family into which he was soon to marry. Still earlier is a family picture in Leningrad showing Jordaens with his parents and his young brothers and sisters.

131 ANTHONY VAN DYCK (1599–1641). Flemish. *The Brazen Serpent.* Painted 1618–20. Oil on canvas, 80¾ x 92½″

Like his compatriot Rubens and the Spaniard Velázquez, Anthony van Dyck was one of the courtier-painters of the seventeenth century, great artists who, because of their personal charm and distinction as well as the high quality of their work, became the favorites and trusted friends of powerful monarchs.

Van Dyck was born in Antwerp and began the study of painting there with Hendrick van Balen. Before he was twenty he entered Rubens' studio, not as an apprentice, but as a skilled assistant to the master. He went to Italy in 1621, probably with the encouragement of Rubens, who had benefited so much from his own long sojourn among Italian artists, and remained there for seven years before he returned to Antwerp.

In 1632 Charles I sent for him to come to England, and there he enjoyed a huge success and was knighted. He worked for a second period in England from 1635 until 1640, creating a style of elegant portrait painting that has since profoundly affected all painters of aristocratic portraits, including even Sargent and Boldini. On Rubens' death in 1640, Van Dyck returned briefly to Flanders and could probably, had he wished, have assumed the direction of the enormously active shop left vacant by Rubens. But Van Dyck, preferring the position he occupied in England, and in any case a very sick man, returned to London, where he died the following year, in 1641.

Van Dyck's painting of *The Brazen Serpent* seems to be an early work, made about 1618–1620, in the harsh, effective manner of the years before he went to Italy. It represents an episode in the Israelites' journey to the Promised Land (Numbers 21:4–9). Having destroyed the Canaanites, they were journeying to Edom by way of the Red Sea, but "the soul of the people was much discouraged because of the way," which was so long and weary and hungry that they complained against their leader and against the Lord. God punished them for their impatience by sending fiery serpents to bite them, and after many people had died, the rest repented and begged Moses to intercede for them. Under the Lord's direction, Moses made a serpent of brass and set it upon a standard, and the sight of this brazen serpent effected a cure for all those who had been bitten. Van Dyck conceived this dramatic miracle as taking place against a sky seething with storm clouds. Moses is pictured at the left holding the standard with the healing serpent before a throng of his injured and miserable, but chastened followers.

132 ANTHONY VAN DYCK (1599–1641). Flemish. *Diana and Endymion Spied upon by a Satyr.* Painted about 1626. Oil on canvas, 56¾ x 64⅛″

Diana alone among the deities of Olympus was supposed to be impervious to the ravages of love, the only goddess, says an old-fashioned writer, who observed perpetual chastity. Her carefree days were spent in outdoor sports, in the company of a train of maidens who were expected to be equally chaste. (It will be remembered, however, that their spotless record was sullied by the pliant Callisto, who yielded to the wooing of the father of the gods.)

Although Diana herself never yielded to the lust of the flesh, in her passionate attachment to the beautiful youth Endymion she must certainly be accused of succumbing to the lust of the eye. She had espied the shepherd—called by some a son of Jove—sleeping in lovely abandon on Mount Latmos, where he fed his flock, and night after night, in her guise of goddess of the moon, descended from Olympus to watch him while he slept. Frequent absences from the home of the gods were not apt to be overlooked by the celestial gossips, who were themselves so experienced in amatory adventure that they

thought the worst of anyone else. Someone took care to bring Diana's lapse to the attention of Jove, who granted to Endymion a choice between a mortal's death and the gift of remaining deathless and ageless, but wrapped in perpetual sleep. Endymion chose to sleep. "Burning Sappho" was the first classical writer to tell the story, which is best known to English readers in the poem of Keats.

In Van Dyck's painting the shepherd and his dog lie fast asleep, and the enamored goddess, too, her quivers abandoned at her side, lies slumbering with her arm entwined in that of her love. In the enchantment of the dark forest a satyr has come up noiselessly at the right, and holds out his hand to surprise and taunt the oblivious pair. The glowing, rippling nude body of Diana (which kept the picture in puritanical retirement for many years) could only have been painted by Van Dyck after his voyage to Italy had begun to free his art from its earlier rigor, and serves to date the picture about 1626.

133 ANTHONY VAN DYCK (1599–1641). Flemish. *Sir Endymion Porter and Van Dyck.* Painted 1632–33. Oil on canvas, 46⅞ x 56¾″

Endymion Porter (1587–1649) was a close friend of Van Dyck, as well as of Rubens. He was born in Spain and brought up by relatives there, serving as a page in the household of the Count-Duke of Olivares. He passed six years in Madrid between 1622 and 1628. Later in England he became Groom of the Bedchamber to King Charles I, who entrusted him with royal missions, and especially with the purchase of works of art for the royal collections, for Porter was a discriminating connoisseur. He remained loyal to Charles in spite of his awareness of the King's misguided conduct. Four years before the execution he went into hiding, emerging only in 1649 after the death of the King, when he attempted to salvage some scrap of his personal fortune, but died himself within the year.

In this oval double portrait, Van Dyck is dressed in the discreetly elegant black costume that the Spanish court had set as a fashionable standard, but Porter wears cloth of silver, richly trimmed with collar and cuffs of pointed lace. Such elaborate petaled cuffs were in style for so brief a period, in 1632 and 1633, that we may safely assume the picture was painted in one of those years. Both gentlemen display the beautiful and aristocratic hands, with exaggeratedly tapering fingers, that characterize most of Van Dyck's fashionable portraits and were very widely imitated in the works of his followers and emulators.

134 PETER PAUL RUBENS (1577–1640). Flemish. *The Judgment of Paris.* Painted 1638–39. Oil on canvas, 78⅜ x 149¼″

At the left of the picture, spurred on by Mercury, who carries his caduceus in one hand and with the other displays the golden prize, Paris sits deeply absorbed. The tense pose and the expression of troubled concentration on the face of the simple shepherd who was elected to choose the fairest of the three competing goddesses evidence only too plainly that he guesses how grave will be the consequences of his decision.

At the extreme right, attended by her peacock, is Juno, with the jeweled crown and purple robe that befit the wife of Olympus' king. Next to Mercury is Minerva, accompanied by her owl, and the only discomfited one of the three. She has thrown her shield and armor to the ground, and though shy, takes a serious part in the contest. Between her sister goddesses, with her little son Cupid clinging to her in an effort to gain her attention, is Venus; a flying *putto* is about to place a crown of flowers on her head, since he, with the prophetic insight of all *amorini*, foresees what decision Paris will make.

In Rubens' picture of the same subject painted about five years earlier and now in London, the figures are amply separated in space; more room intervenes between the men and the goddesses, and the three lovely women themselves are clearly detached from one another. In the Prado version, on the other hand, Rubens has integrated the composition in countless ways: Mercury's hand holding the golden apple of discord almost brushes Minerva's scarf; Venus' vermilion robe touches Minerva's thigh; and the elbow of Juno pushes forward in front of Venus' arm.

After the commission for this painting had been given, Rubens was delayed by one of his tormenting attacks of gout, which became increasingly painful toward the end of his life. In February of 1639, however, Philip IV received a letter from his brother, the Cardinal-Infante Ferdinand of Austria, who wrote from Antwerp: *"The Judgment of Paris* is finished. According to all the painters it is the best work Rubens has painted,—only one fault . . . the three goddesses are too nude. The Venus quite evidently is a portrait of his own wife, who is unquestionably the best there is around here today."

135 Andrea Mantegna (1431–1506). Italian. *The Dormition of the Virgin.* Painted about 1462. Tempera on wood, 21¼ x 16½"

The story of the Dormition of the Virgin is apocryphal. Mary was warned by the Archangel Michael of her approaching end and sent out a call for the Apostles. Miraculously, all but St. Thomas were able to be present. In Mantegna's picture St. John is honored in bearing the palm which announces her death, but the belief is that she did not die, but merely fell asleep to await the Resurrection.

Mantegna's *Dormition of the Virgin* is a diminutive work but a great one and a credit to Philip IV's connoisseurship. It is one of the Prado's very few Italian paintings of the fifteenth century. The painting is a triumph of serenity, the eleven figures being so placed about the recumbent Virgin that they do not crowd the small space, but with bowed heads add to the solemn stillness of the scene. One

of the Apostles is administering the rites for the dying, assisted by two of the others.

From the wide open window of the Castello di Corte in Mantua, in which Mantegna laid his scene, a blue sky and the still waters of Lago del Mezzo and Lago Inferiore separated by the bridge of San Giorgio lead to the open country side. The composition attains its sense of peace by the deliberate use of horizontals and verticals. The open window is framed by heavy columns, resting upon the tessellated floor, and a chain of white clouds in the sky parallels the horizon and the window ledge. The painting, made about 1462, belonged to Vincenzo Gonzaga and later, in 1627, was sold to Charles I of England with a large group of art from the Gonzaga collections. Philip IV bought it through his ambassador when the Commonwealth sold Charles's belongings in 1649.

The Italian scholar Roberto Longhi (in an article in *Pan*, 1934) has recognized a fragmentary panel, 10¾" high, in the Vendeghini collection in Ferrara as by Mantegna and evidently the upper portion of the Prado's panel. It represents Christ in a glory, surrounded by angels, receiving the doll-like Soul of the Virgin, a usual feature of the Dormition subject. Added at the top of the Prado *Dormition* it would give a composition strikingly like Mantegna's early mosaic in the Cappella dei Mascoli in Venice, which depicts a lofty interior with Christ high above the bed of the expiring Virgin.

Andrea Mantegna was born in 1431 and as a child was adopted by Squarcione, the great Paduan teacher who was influenced by classical sculpture. Mantegna was influenced also by Donatello's sculptures and by the great drawings of the Venetian artist, Jacopo Bellini, whose daughter, Nicolosia, he married. About 1459–60 he painted frescoes in the Eremitani Chapel in Padua, which were ruined in World War II. Mantegna was one of the very great Italian painters. His imposing figures in classic draperies, drawn with almost harsh incisiveness, were a powerful influence on a number of important painters who followed him, such as Cosimo Tura, Carlo Crivelli, and the young Giovanni Bellini.

136 Raphael (Raffaello Sanzio; 1483–1520). Italian. *Portrait of a Cardinal.* Painted about 1510. Oil on wood, 31⅛ x 24"

In his brief career, Raphael attained to an excellence in his paintings of Madonnas, of portraits, and of mural decorations which has made him the most prominent representative of the Italian Renaissance style. Probably no other artist of the period achieved in so short a time such mastery over his art and such entire approval from the influential people of his day.

An Umbrian by birth, he received his earliest training in Urbino, but was no more than sixteen when he worked in Perugia as assistant to Perugino, who formed his early style. Five years later, in 1504, he visited Florence and encountered there influences from the more progressive school of painting which permanently modified his earlier man-

ner. About 1509 he went to Rome, and from this time on until his early death filled commissions for the papacy, decorating the walls and ceilings of the Vatican, serving as first architect of St. Peter's, and during his first years in Rome recording in tranquil, imperturbable portraits the appearance of many members of the papal court.

The subject of this arresting portrait has not been identified. Among the many names of cardinals suggested, that of Ippolito d'Este the son of Alfonso I of Ferrara, seems the most probable; the thin, curving nose is at least a characteristic of the Este family. The picture has the satisfying decorative beauty of all Raphael's greatest portraits—a carefully balanced filling of the picture space, in which the design of the silhouette is lovely in itself, and a delineation of the forms by means of sure and simple planes. But primarily the portrait's unforgettable quality is due to the unfathomable meaning in the exquisitely refined and weary face. The large, wide-set eyes are intent on some distant prospect, and the subtle lines of the mouth are shut in unyielding reticence.

137 Raphael (Raffaello Sanzio; 1483–1520). Italian. *The Madonna of the Fish.* Painted about 1513. Oil on canvas, 84⅝ x 62¼"

Raphael's greatest Roman Madonnas, among which this and the Sistine Madonna are surely to be counted, present a paradox in their combination of humanity with religious majesty. The Virgin here is a very credible tender mother, barefoot and simply clothed, looking graciously on her worshipers, but at the same time raised above the level of the earth and set apart from the spectator by the architectural block, symmetrically placed in the center of the foreground. She is apparently in the very act of turning away from St. Jerome and his lion toward the group at the left, for her body still turns a little toward St. Jerome, and the Child still holds fast to the Saint's book. The gentle Archangel Raphael, young and reverent, has sought the Virgin's attention in order to present his kneeling charge, young Tobias, who carries by a string the medicinal fish that the angel helped him to catch as a remedy for his father's blindness.

Two drawings preceding this painting are preserved, one in the Uffizi, and one (formerly the property of the painter, Sir Thomas Lawrence) in a private collection in England. They show how Raphael's mind worked. Both Tobias and the angel began as contemporary, very earthy boys, probably studio apprentices, but as the artist's scheme evolved into a great composition he introduced increasing piety. As early as 1524, the painting is mentioned in a chapel dedicated to St. Rosa in the Church of San Domenico at Naples.

138 Titian (Tiziano Vecelli; 1477–1576). Italian. *Bacchanal.* Painted about 1518. Signed on the blouse of the reclining woman:

Ticianus F. No. 101. Oil on canvas, 68⅞ x 76"

This *Bacchanal* by Titian together with his *Worship of Venus*, also in the Prado (plate 139) and the pagan *Bacchus and Ariadne* in the National Gallery in London, which Titian painted a few years later, were all ordered by Alfonso d'Este (1486–1534) for his studio in the castle at Ferrara. Vasari in his life of Titian stated that Bellini's *Feast of the Gods*, painted in 1514 (the superlative work now in Washington) was also installed in the studio, but that this was an error has been demonstrated by Edgar Wind in his *Bellini's Feast of the Gods* (1948).

Alfonso's sister Isabella d'Este had ordered made for her an Italian translation of the *Imagines,* by Philostratus, and from this book which he had borrowed from her, Alfonso worked out in detail the subject of the Bacchanal which Titian was to paint. Alfonso is said to have wished a figure put into the painting which would recall the draped classical sculpture of Ariadne, yet the locale had to be the island of Andros instead of Naxos, where the Greek poets had left Ariadne asleep, for Alfonso liked playing anagrams (Andriae and Ariadne!), and Titian was prudent enough to congratulate him on his proficiency in the game. But whatever artless sixteenth-century thoughts may have conditioned the subject matter, the result achieved by Titian is the purest and most blissful pagan poetry.

Dalliance on this enchanted sylvan isle, set in the warm blue Aegean, was made doubly agreeable by the copious spring flowing with wine, shown by Titian in the left foreground. In the nearer center is a handsome nymph in red with fashionably waved coiffure. It is a portrait of Violante, Titian's lady-love. She wears her usual device consisting of two violets in her bosom (together here with Titian's signature) and another violet behind her ear. A glorious portrait of her by Palma Vecchio is in the Vienna museum, and she is thought to have been Palma's daughter. It was the art historian, Molmenti, who made the naive discovery that this relationship was impossible because Palma was not a married man!

Violante in the Prado's painting is reaching automatically for more wine. She holds also a small flute, and on the sheet of music lying before her on the ground is a French *ronde:* "He that takes a drink and doesn't drink again, doesn't truly know what drinking is."

Titian's *Bacchanal,* together with his *Worship of Venus,* is thought to have been given to Philip IV by Nicolò Ludovisi of Rome, the Count of Monterrey carrying it to Spain with him when his term as Viceroy of Rome had ended.

139 TITIAN (TIZIANO VECELLI; 1477–1576). Italian. *The Worship of Venus.* Painted about 1518. Signed on cloth in center: *No. 102 Di Ticianus F.* Oil on canvas, 67¾ x 68⅞"

The theme of this painting, like that of its companion, the *Bacchanal* (plate 138), was suggested by a passage from Philostratus.

The brief passage in the *Imagines* (I:6) associated with this *Worship of Venus* had already been visualized for Alfonso d'Este by Fra Bartolommeo (died 1517) in a drawing, which was, however, very different from Titian's except that both show the nymph at the right offering Venus a mirror.

Titian's Venus, though a mere graven image, seems to look upon her worshipers with satisfaction. Happy *putti* throw down apples from the tree, and countless other *putti* on the ground, those not completely engrossed with pre-puppy love, eat and enjoy them. This is the first stage of love, the Chaotic stage, according to the Neoplatonists, whereas in the *Bacchanal* the adults are sufficiently advanced to engage in Harmonious Love. Finally, *Bacchus and Ariadne* (National Gallery, London), completed in 1523, is an illustration of Transcendent or Divine Love, in which an immortal takes part, thus inevitably and promptly leading to the demise of the mortal partner.

This painting, also called *Offering to the Goddess of Love,* and painted at Titian's comparatively youthful age of forty, has the same history as the *Bacchanal.* It was perhaps planned a year or two earlier but was painted at about the same time. The *Worship of Venus* has the same height as the *Bacchanal* and *Bacchus and Ariadne.* Its width today is, however, about seven inches less, and indeed it is only too evident that the ends of the canvas cut off the extreme figures in a markedly unsatisfactory way.

In these poetic pastorals, Titian says a farewell to the spirit of his colleague, Giorgione, as the style in his painting takes the direction which is to continue for another half-century.

140 TITIAN (TIZIANO VECELLI; 1477–1576). Italian. *Charles V on Horseback at the Battle of Mühlberg.* Painted 1548. Oil on canvas, 130¾ x 97⅞"

In 1548 the Emperor spent several months in Augsburg, and was joined there by Titian. The portrait of Charles in armor, carrying a lance and mounted on a dark brown horse, is a major work. It celebrates the strategy and leadership of Charles V in the Battle of Mühlberg, not far from Leipzig. Here, on April 24, 1547, he outmaneuvered his Protestant opponents, defeating their armies and taking captive their leader, Johann Friedrich of Saxony.

Titian's portrait conveys its mood with extraordinary power. Gustavo Frizzoni, the art historian, called it the world's greatest portrait, and in any case it is unique in sentiment. Emerging from a forest onto a plain lit by a sky streaked with wild sunset clouds, Charles's bearing expresses the pride of victory and latent power. His face wears the look of a vehement personality which seems to carry the urge of activity and ambition to the very farthest boundaries of sanity. He still has ten years of life ahead, but already he is living on his nerve.

141 TITIAN (TIZIANO VECELLI; 1477–1576). Italian. *Danaë and the Shower of Gold.* Painted 1552–54. Oil on canvas, 50¾ x 70⅞"

According to the classical myth, Danaë, a lovely and well-born young woman, was kept imprisoned by her father because an oracle had foretold that he would be slain by her son. Thus lonely Danaë could become acquainted with no mortal man. But Jove, ever aware of the beautiful women among mortals, learned of Danaë and, disguised as a golden shower, visited her in her prison. Their son, the famous Perseus, later killed Danaë's father by accident when they were throwing quoits together, and thus the prophecy was fulfilled.

In Titian's *Danaë* at the Prado, the sky is filled with tumultuous clouds as the golden particles rain down. Nothing could conceivably be in stronger contrast than the mood of Danaë dissolved in a dream of love, and that of her crude maid servant, avidly reaching for the falling gold simply because of its purchasing power. Yet the painting with its rich, fused tonality and its miraculously resolved component parts is a perfect harmony.

It was offered to Philip II by Titian in a letter of March 23, 1553, in which he referred to it as one of his *poesias.* About eight years earlier he had painted a lovely *Danaë,* the one now in the Naples Gallery, in which there is no maid servant but a surprised cupid looking back at the showery sky. The body of Danaë is more precisely modeled than in the later picture, and her face wears a less dreamy, less sensuous expression; she scarcely seems aware of the golden rain.

142 TITIAN (TIZIANO VECELLI; 1477–1576). Italian. *The Entombment.* Painted 1559. Signed on a flat stone leaning against the tomb: *Titianus Vecellius Aeques.* Oil on canvas, 53⅞ x 68⅞"

In this perfectly conceived and executed work of his old age, Titian has balanced his movement, softened his outlines, and dematerialized his forms to a point where his painting seems almost to be an expression of emotion without any vehicle. According to Georg Gronau as quoted in the catalogue of the Prado, "Human sorrow has never been expressed in a more sensitive and essentially artistic manner."

The figures, fused into the entire tonality and compositional unity though they are, have their clearly expressed functions and forces. The old Joseph of Arimathea is thought to be a portrait of Titian himself (he was then eighty-two). The cloudlike body of Mary Magdalene has the spirituality of an angel. More than one critic has examined the contrast between this *Entombment* and the artist's treatment of the same subject in the Louvre, painted thirty-four years earlier. There, for all the beauty of its color and of its separate parts, there is far less unity of movement and light.

143 Attributed to GIORGIONE (1478–1510). Italian. *The Virgin with St. Anthony and St. Roch.* Painted about 1510. Oil on canvas, 36¼ x 52⅜"

The authorship of this painting has been much disputed. It is unfinished but well preserved. The elegance of the composition, the grace of the contours, and the sympathetic tone of the whole are characteristic of Giorgione. According to the critic Georg Martin Richter, it belongs to the painter's last period, and the flowers on the curtain behind the Virgin are the insignia of the Loredan family. A member of that family had earlier commissioned Giorgione to paint a fresco (now lost) on the façade of the Loredan palace in Venice.

About 1650 the Duke of Medina de las Torres, Viceroy of Naples, gave *The Virgin with St. Anthony and St. Roch* to Philip IV, and Velázquez set it as an overdoor in the Sacristy of the Escorial. At that time, the painting was attributed to Pordenone. Some modern critics, however, have believed that Giorgione was its author, while others have inclined to Titian. Still others have accepted neither attribution, and in his catalogue of the Prado, Sánchez Cantón remarks, "It is an eloquent example of the vacillations of the critics."

This profusion of critical opinions is perhaps an index of the importance of the painting. On the other hand, this picture is by no means the only one which has received the treatment of a medicine-ball snatched by adherents of Giorgione and those of Titian. The two Venetian contemporaries, equally gigantic in their genius, had undergone the same schooling with Giovanni Bellini. There are paintings, known to be Giorgione's, in a new style, with poetic figures drenched in the beauty of the landscapes they inhabit. Young Titian learned much from his equally young companion, but it is only their early works which can be confused. In the case of Giorgione, early works are, alas, all that we have, for he died at the age of thirty-three—whereas Titian lived to thrice thirty-three.

144 RAPHAEL SCHOOL (Sixteenth Century). Italian. *The Holy Family ("La Perla")* Painted about 1518. Oil on wood, 56¾ x 45¼"

This richly fascinating picture was painted not very long before Raphael's tragically premature death. The design is usually conceded to be his, but many critics see in the execution the style of Raphael's assistant and immediate follower, Giulio Romano, and perhaps also a little of the less gifted helper in his shop, the pedestrian Penni.

The complex interlocking of the four figures in the foreground, and the foreshortened rocking-cradle that begins the skillful recession into great depth, are elements very foreign indeed to Raphael's earlier classic style, and suggest what directions his art might have taken had he lived on.

Few paintings have passed through the hands of more distinguished successive owners than this *Holy Family*. Painted for the Bishop of Bayeux, Count Lodovico da Canossa, it was acquired at the beginning of the seventeenth century by Vincenzo Gonzaga, the Duke of Mantua. In 1627 the Gonzaga collection was bought by King Charles I of England. When Charles was beheaded in 1649, the Commonwealth auctioned his works of art, and Philip IV's ambassador bought this painting for him. The picture acquired its flattering name "*La Perla*" at this time, for Philip on seeing it is said to have exclaimed that it was the pearl of his collection, and in 1654 gave it a place of honor over the high altar of the Sacristy at the Escorial. Joseph Bonaparte carried it off to Paris for several years, but it was restored to the Escorial in 1822, and from there was moved to the Prado.

145 ANDREA DEL SARTO (1486–1531). *Portrait of a Woman* (The Artist's Wife?). Painted about 1520. Oil on wood, 28¾ x 22"

Although the identification is by no means sure, it is tempting to see in the features of this well-favored but sultry Florentine lady the likeness of Lucrezia del Fede, whom Vasari blamed for so many of Andrea del Sarto's misdemeanors. The woman portrayed here can be recognized again and again as the model for the Madonna in Andrea's religious paintings, notably in the Uffizi's *Madonna of the Harpies* and *The Charity* in the Louvre.

Lucrezia was a widow when Andrea, at the age of thirty-one, married her. He had been a pupil of Piero di Cosimo in his native city of Florence, and since 1508 a member of the painters' guild. In 1518, the year after his marriage, Andrea, who had already shown great talents in the execution of large frescoes as well as panels, was called to France by Francis I. After a year of deferential treatment at the French court, he succeeded, by promising a speedy return in getting the king's permission to revisit Florence and his frivolous young wife. Whether or not it was really she, as Vasari maliciously asserts, who seduced her husband into extravagances that ate up all the money entrusted to him by Francis I for the purchase of works of art, it is certain that Andrea never went back to France.

Although he was an excellent artist, who composed large pictures in the High Renaissance style and went on to the asymmetry of the next development, and though he trained in his studio such important painters as Pontormo, Il Rosso, and the historian-painter Vasari himself, Andrea del Sarto's art is characterized by an indefinable excess of competence which has tagged him with the slightly denigrating nickname, "the faultless painter."

146 PARMIGIANINO (FRANCESCO MAZZOLA; 1503–40). Italian. *Portrait of the Count of San Secondo.* Painted 1533–35. Oil on wood, 52⅜ x 38⅝"

The Italian Pier Maria Rossi, Count of San Secondo (1504–47), bore the same name as his father. He had a brief but active career as a free-lance army commander or *condottiere*. In this capacity he served the Emperor Charles V and also the Emperor's disturbing rival, the French king, Francis I. He is reputed to have been as handsome as his portrait by Parmigianino shows him. Indeed (according to Sydney J. Freedberg in his monograph on the artist), Federico Rossi, the son of the *condottiere*, praised the portrait as a likeness, and there is also a medal portraying him which is said to resemble the painted portrait in the Prado.

In the painting the Count is represented as no more than thirty years old, yet already a man of splendid presence, not to mention his unusually luxurious and well-groomed beard. The portrait is thought to have been painted in Parma, the city which gave Parmigianino his nickname.

The real name of the artist, whose career was even briefer than that of the Count himself, was Francesco Mazzola. Deeply influenced as a youth by Correggio, he was active in Rome and Bologna from about 1522 until 1531, and was again at work in Parma almost until his death at the age of thirty-seven. He painted distinguished religious pictures carrying Correggio's style well over into Mannerism, but his portraits with their combined charm and aristocratic poise are more immediately enjoyed.

147 VERONESE (PAOLO CALIARI; 1528?–88). Italian. *Venus and Adonis.* Painted about 1580. Oil on canvas, 83½ x 75¼"

This rich and glorious canvas, typical of the late work of Veronese, is one of the treasures of Venetian painting that Velázquez bought in Italy in 1651 to enhance the royal collections. The painter, whose real name was Paolo Caliari, derives his nickname from Verona, whence he came. Soon after the middle of the sixteenth century he was established in Venice as one of the greatest painters of his time, decorating the halls of the Doge's palace, furnishing altarpieces and decorations for the sumptuous Venetian churches, and recording in splendid portraits the dignitaries of his day.

He painted this picture of *Venus and Adonis* about 1580, more than a quarter century after Titian had painted the same subject and sent it off to Philip II. This version, however, differs from Titian's, from Rubens' later famous handling of the same theme, and from Veronese's own earlier renderings of the subject, which show Venus' tearful and futile efforts to detain her hunter-lover from the chase which she knows will cost his life.

Veronese instead depicts here a brief, idyllic moment in the story: Adonis, lulled with contentment, lies with his head on Venus' lap, one relaxed hand resting on his hunting horn. Only the dogs are watchful, and Cupid desperately tries to prevent one of them from waking Adonis, who sleeps on through the deepening sunset, while the beautiful blonde goddess guards his slumber with her fan and shields him with the curve of her pearly body.

148 FEDERIGO BAROCCI (1526–1612). Italian. *The Nativity.* Painted about 1605. Oil on canvas, 52¾ x 51⅜″

Federigo Barocci spent most of his long and productive life in Urbino. As a young man he had learned a great deal by studying the fine works of art in the collections of the dukes of Urbino; he also studied painting in Pesaro with his uncle, Bartolommeo Genga. Cardinal Giulio della Rovere and Pope Paul IV employed him on commissions in Rome. Barocci's style was strongly influenced by the art of Correggio, but his contours retain more definition, and in his gentle types and fresh, delicate color a markedly personal note can be perceived.

The Nativity must be one of his later works, painted about 1605, for the position of the *Bambino* and the improvised bedding in which he lies, with the coverlet turned back from his swaddling clothes, appear again in the portrait of the baby Duke of Urbino (which bears that date) in the Uffizi in Florence. But in that portrait of the little Federigo the brocades and embroideries befitting ducal splendor stiffen not only the cradle but the painter's brush, and the painting lacks entirely the lyric poetry of the Prado *Nativity.* This tender mood is evoked by the flitting light emanating from the baby Jesus in his manger bed, and also by the gesture of St. Joseph, who seems at once to point out the Child and his radiant, adoring Mother, and to protect his family from the intrusion of the shepherd who has come inquiring at the slightly opened door.

149 ARTEMISIA GENTILESCHI (1597–1651). Italian. *A Peasant Girl with Pigeons.* Painted about 1630. Oil on canvas, 23⅝ x 18½″

Although this painting has often been called a self-portrait by Artemisia, the identification does not seem confirmed either by comparison with the supposed self-portrait at Hampton Court or with the engraved and probably reliable portrait of the artist that Sandrart made less than a generation after her death. The pastoral motif of the pigeons furthermore strikes a note completely out of harmony with the legend that has grown up around Artemisia.

She was the pupil of her father Orazio Gentileschi, one of the more elegant and refined followers of Caravaggio, and of the painter Agostino Tassi. Her early life was spent in Rome, but after 1621 she and her father lived for five years in Tuscany, chiefly in Florence, and then for about seven in Naples. Orazio died around 1638, and the following year the young woman was in London, where she built up for herself a considerable reputation as a painter of portraits. The last ten or eleven years of her life were spent in Naples, executing important commissions for large-scale paintings in which she showed herself a strong artist, in various respects the superior of many of her masculine contemporaries.

Her temperament welcomed the natural-ism with which Caravaggio had revolutionized the sterile academic Italian tradition of the end of the sixteenth century, and her own intense dramatic proclivities converted this naturalism into violent expression. Her best-known works are the gory paintings of Judith cutting off the head of Holophernes, evidences of a powerful primitive force in herself that contrasts strangely with the legends of her extraordinary personal charm in appearance and conversation. Artemisia Gentileschi surely can be called the most important woman painter before the French Vigée Lebrun in the following century.

150 GIOVANNI BATTISTA TIEPOLO (1696–1770). Italian. Fragment: *An Angel Bearing a Monstrance.* Painted 1769. Oil on canvas, 72⅞ x 70⅛″

This is only the top half of a canvas painted for the high altar of San Pascual at Aranjuez before August 1769, recording the vision of San Pascual Baylon in which he saw an angel descending from heaven to present him with the Eucharist in a monstrance. Doubtless on royal orders, or at any rate with permission, the painter Mengs soon tore down the altarpiece, cutting it in half, and himself made a new painting for the altar not long after Tiepolo's death in 1770. The Prado has an oil sketch for the entire composition, and also the lower part, showing St. Pascual kneeling. In the upper half, reproduced here, the angel descends from heaven and is seen before a classical church and the walls of a convent garden, presumably at the monastery of San Pascual Baylon.

The saint was born in Aragon on May 24, 1540, the feast of Pentecost, and died also on the feast of Pentecost on May 17, 1592. In his younger years he was a shepherd, and even as a child was devoted to the Eucharist. At about the age of twenty-four he was received by the Franciscan friars as a lay brother, and in 1564 took the habit of St. Francis, spending most of his life as a humble doorkeeper in different Spanish convents. He was amiable and modest, and all his life was filled with love for the Holy Eucharist. He was canonized in 1690.

Tiepolo, that amazing flare-up of genius in a Venice that seemed spent, was invited to Madrid by Charles III. He arrived there on June 7, 1762 with his son, Domenico, and another assistant, and worked on the frescoes in the Royal Palace, completing them in 1767. He then began seven paintings ordered by King Charles for the church of San Pascual at Aranjuez, finishing them in 1769, the year before his death.

151 TITIAN (TIZIANO VECELLI; 1477–1576). Italian. *St. Margaret.* Painted about 1565. Signed at the left on a level with the Saint's head: TITIANUS. Oil on canvas, 95¼ x 71⅝″

Against a ravishing landscape lit by the subdued glow of early evening the graceful figure of St. Margaret emerges, holding in her left hand a small cross which has magical power capable of subduing the evil dragon at her feet. The figure of the Saint with her swaying movement is one of Titian's loveliest. Wonderful too is the dark landscape with its rocks and trees more guessed at than seen, and its dark water leading the eye to the distant town.

About St. Margaret we have more poetic myth than solid history. In the crabbed words of a Vatican historian, "Her existence seems assured, but her acts are a forgery."

152 TITIAN (TIZIANO VECELLI; 1477–1576). Italian. *Religion Succored by Spain.* Painted 1534; reworked about 1572. Signed on the stone, near the cross: *Titianus. F.* Oil on canvas, 66⅛ x 66⅛″

Visitors to the Prado should not feel humiliated if at first the significance of this gorgeous painting seems to escape them. Titian's original intention as to the subject seems to be unknown today. In its first and unfinished form the picture was seen by Vasari when he visited Titian's studio in 1566, but unfortunately he failed to inquire of Titian what the subject was. However there can be no doubt that this is the painting which Vasari saw and described in his *Lives* as follows: "He also began, many years ago for Alfonso I, Duke of Ferrara, a picture of a nude woman bowing before Minerva with another figure alongside, and the sea in the middle of which, in the distance, is Neptune in his car."

Alfonso died in 1534, but after the smashing victory of the Spanish and Venetian fleets at Lepanto in 1571, Titian took up the canvas again—his interest possibly stimulated by Vasari's praise of it. Minerva was given a banner for her spear and thus became the personification of Spain, and her adjutant, supplied with a sword, became Justice. The poor, cringing woman, upon whom Minerva had been visiting a goddess' awesome punishment, needed no alteration to convert her to The Church beyond a blue drapery, a chalice, a small cross resting against the rock at her feet, and a number of threatening heretical snakes squirming behind her. The distant Neptune in his car was given a turban, thus typifying the Turkish sea power. In 1575 the painting was sent to Philip II, the most likely man in all the world to appreciate such a subject.

153 TITIAN (TIZIANO VECELLI; 1477–1576). Italian. *The Fall of Man.* Painted about 1570. Signed on stone at lower left: *Titianus F.* Oil on canvas, 94½ x 73¼″

The sumptuousness of this painting of the Temptation, painted by Titian in his nineties, marks in a sense the last phase of the Renaissance. When Rubens copied it almost sixty years later (plate 121), he found the woman's body and the man's likewise somewhat too spare and too rigid for his taste, but requiring no fundamental changes to convert the picture into a fine and characteristic Baroque Rubens.

In 1787, Richard Cumberland, the English traveler, in his *Accurate and Descriptive Catalogue* of paintings in the Palace at Madrid, described the pictures in the king's antechamber, where he found what he called an *Adam and Eve in Paradise* by Titian, and in the same room the copy by Rubens. Rubens, he observed, gave the figures a "broader nakedness. . . . Titian's figures never wore clothes, whereas in Rubens' copy of the same, persons appear to have laid theirs aside and exposed themselves to shame for the benefit of the painter."

154 TINTORETTO (JACOPO ROBUSTI; 1518–94). Italian. *Judith About to Slay Holophernes.* Painted about 1550. Oil on canvas, 22⅞ x 46⅞"

Tintoretto, or "little dyer," was called this because of his father's trade; his real name was Jacopo Robusti. He was born in Venice and passed almost all of his long, intensely productive life there. Though he appears to have studied briefly with Titian, he was largely self-taught, setting as his aim the combination of the coloring of Titian with the drawing of Michelangelo, who impressed him greatly.

This sparkling little scene, like *Joseph and Potiphar's Wife* (plate 155), belongs to a group of six panels in the Prado originally designed to ornament the sloping cove of a ceiling, which had as its central decoration *The Purification of the Midianite Virgins,* also in the Prado. Palomino, the eighteenth-century biographer of Velázquez, records that the painter on his second voyage to Italy bought for King Philip IV a series of ceiling paintings by Tintoretto with stories from the Old Testament and these paintings must certainly be the ones to which he refers.

The scene divides into two sharply contrasted halves. At the left, all is tension and motion: the unexpectedly youthful servant stands poised with the bag which in a moment is to receive the severed head of Holophernes; Judith draws back the curtain and aims the sword; the clouds race upward to hide the crescent moon as though the attainment of this objective were the signal for the act. The right half of the picture employs the sloping downward lines of the drapery and the relaxed members of the doomed tyrant to emphasize the heavy drunken oblivion in which he approaches his end. Nowhere have Tintoretto's agile flashing brush and inspired draftsmanship achieved a greater effect of the rich, shimmering play of light and shadow. The grimness of the subject with its passionately emotional content is altogether subordinated to the charm and dexterity of the dainty female figures, so skillfully contrasted with the great nude male.

155 TINTORETTO (JACOPO ROBUSTI; 1518–94). Italian. *Joseph and Potiphar's Wife.* Painted about 1550. Oil on canvas, 21¼ x 46⅛"

This brilliant little panel, like *Judith About to Slay Holophernes* (plate 154), belonged to the series of six ceiling decorations that Velázquez bought in Italy for the royal Spanish collections. These small Biblical scenes, which must date from about 1550, are less developed in style, to be sure, but clearly foreshadow the marvelous decorations of the Scuola di San Rocco. The firmness of Joseph's resolve as he attempts to resist the wiles of the lascivious wife of Potiphar (see detail, plate 156) tips him backward at an angle that parallels the exaggerated perspective of the architecture, clearly meant to be looked at from below.

156 TINTORETTO (JACOPO ROBUSTI; 1518–94). Italian. *Joseph and Potiphar's Wife* (detail of plate 155)

Probably nowhere in the history of art before the painting of Boucher has a diminutive nude been charged with so much insolence and unabashed wickedness as the artist has concentrated in the wife of Potiphar. Large-eyed, with bangs and double chin, she exerts all of her feminine will and ripe charms to detain the chaste and youthful Joseph.

157 TINTORETTO (JACOPO ROBUSTI; 1518–94). Italian. *Gentleman with a Gold Chain.* Painted about 1550. Oil on canvas, 40½ x 29⅞"

When Tintoretto painted portraits, his keenness and psychological penetration were always mellowed by a warm human sympathy with the subject, so that his likenesses present the spectator with a startlingly vivid presence. The costume is usually, as here, sufficiently generalized and dark to concentrate attention on the hands and the moving expression in the eyes.

It has been suggested that we have in this exceptionally beautiful portrait a likeness of the painter's contemporary, Paolo Veronese. If the picture were painted about 1550, as some critics believe, Veronese, whose birth date is unfortunately not certain, would probably have been in his early twenties—an age which scarcely accords with the maturity and experience in his bearded face, with its already receding hairline. Our efforts to find out what Veronese really looked like are not helped very much by comparison with the figure some regard as a self-portrait, the debonair huntsman with his hounds in the decoration of the Villa Maser. The head of a musician in the center of the Louvre's *Marriage at Cana,* however, and the profile of a man silhouetted against the left-hand column in the *Feast in the House of Levi* in the Academy at Venice, are also called self-portraits of Veronese, and with some probability. To these the wise and courteous gentleman of the Prado portrait does indeed bear a resemblance.

158 VERONESE (PAOLO CALIARI; 1528?–88). Italian. *Moses Saved from the Nile.* Painted about 1575. Oil on canvas, 19⅝ x 16⅞"

Like the Prado's *Venus and Adonis* (plate 147), this small, exquisite picture is rather late in Veronese's career, probably about 1575. In painting Biblical subjects, the artist made no attempt whatsoever to employ generalized or simplified costume and architecture to suggest earlier times and distant lands. Frankly bewitched by the brilliant opulence of his beloved Venice, he saw no reason to deprive the people in his paintings of all the splendor they would have enjoyed if they too had inhabited his city.

So it is that we find Pharoah's daughter and her attendants dressed in the brocades and jewels of Venetian ladies. A handsome Moor in the foreground, wearing an earring, and a richly dressed dwarf at the right provide the touches of glamour and exoticism that made life on the lagoons so varied. The town glimpsed beyond the arches of the bridge over the Nile is likewise patently an Italian, not a Biblical, city, with close-packed houses and a towering campanile. As in so many of Veronese's paintings, the landscape background, though itself rich in its forms of foliage and clouds, serves as an enchanting foil for the diversity and lushness of the main subject.

159 TINTORETTO (JACOPO ROBUSTI; 1518–94). Italian. *A Battle Between Turks and Christians.* Painted about 1580. Oil on canvas, 73¼ x 121"

This picture, which is another of those bought by Velázquez in Italy, has long been popularly known as *The Rape of Helen,* because of the recumbent figure of the fair captive in the left foreground, over whose form one of the victors is drawing a concealing drapery. It is probable, however, that the seizure of beautiful women was regarded as a traditional aspect of a military triumph, and the occurrence of the motif is thus not necessarily a classical allusion.

Battle scenes commemorating Venetian victories were among Tintoretto's often-repeated subjects; in the Great Council Hall of the Doge's Palace in Venice there are four such, and in another hall of the same Palace there is the marvelously violent and clashing *Siege of Zara.*

In 1562 Tintoretto painted for Cardinal Ercole Gonzaga a picture showing a battle with the Turks, but the style of the Prado picture suggests a date nearly two decades later. The space is arranged with great skill, defined and accented with intersecting diagonals. The foreground figures are large and imminent, looming before the spectator like actors seen from the first row of the orchestra; the panorama of the fleeing enemy, with horses charging through the water, victims drowning, and the broken ranks on the distant shore, is painted in small scale and in a lighter key, and shows clearly why Tintoretto's technique in this painting has been likened to a tapestry.

160 NICOLAS POUSSIN (1594–1665). French. *Bacchic Scene*. Painted 1632–36. Oil on canvas, 29⅛ x 23⅝"

Nicolas Poussin, the classicist and one of the very greatest of all French painters, demonstrates admirably the difference between an ordinary eclectic and a learned genius who achieved to perfection in his painting the integration of his deep knowledge of classical art and literature with his profound feeling for form and order. He was born in Normandy, where he began the study of art with an unimportant French painter. Before he was twenty he transferred to Paris and entered on his lifelong apprenticeship to classism by studying prints after Raphael and his followers that were to be seen there. He went to Florence about 1620 and four years later settled in Rome, where he remained for the rest of his life.

This voluntary exile from France was broken only once, by a trip to Paris from 1640 to 1642. In Rome he continued his study of Raphael and examined the work of Annibale Carracci and Domenichino, which had proceeded from the art of Raphael. Titian also interested him and influenced some of his most delightful early works. Most of all, however, his serious attention was devoted to classical sculpture and architecture and to the classical literature necessary for their understanding and interpretation.

He developed an inspired landscape style based on his own copious drawings, but never directly on nature, which according to the canon of his art had to be deliberately reorganized and composed. Poussin painted subjects from the Bible (see plate 161), but his most splendid and heroic pictures are mythological. His nobility and measured elegance, which find parallels in the writings of Racine and Corneille, are always truly French in spirit.

The shallow depth of the contained space in this *Bacchic Scene*, and the ornamental design of the figures against a relatively simple ground, suggest that Poussin here took his inspiration from classical reliefs. There are few figures: a nude nymph sits in profile at the left, holding a pitcher with replenishment for the low wine bowl on the ground beside her. She is accompanied in these very subdued and dignified revels by an ivy-crowned and ivy-girdled satyr, pictured in the act of drinking from a jug which a cupid or *putto* steadies for him.

161 NICOLAS POUSSIN (1594–1665). French. *The Triumph of David*. Painted 1625–30. Oil on canvas, 39⅜ x 51⅛"

This picture is a Greek or Roman translation of an Old Testament subject. It is one of Poussin's completely satisfying works, combining perfect semi-nude human forms in restrained motion, indeed nearly static, with a setting of ancient architecture and harmonious landscape. The triumphant young hero sits in introspection beside the armor and the horrid head of the gigantic Philistine bully Goliath, whom he has just killed. He leans on the giant's long sword which he had used for the beheading. Winged Victory stands beside him, about to bestow the hero's crown of laurel, while a cupid hands her in addition a crown of gold, in prophecy of his later kingship. Two other cupids are playing with David's harp. The lowly sling which felled the giant is nowhere to be seen in this stately delineation. In Spain simple shepherds still use slings to head off their flocks or drive away wild dogs.

Poussin must have painted this work about 1625 to 1630, when he was in his thirties. He died at seventy-one. The painting was described in detail by Bellori in 1672, when it belonged to Cardinal Girolamo Casamata. Later both this picture and the *Bacchic Scene* (plate 160) belonged to the Roman painter Carlo Maratti. King Philip V of Spain bought them from his heirs in 1724, and in the middle of the eighteenth century they were among the ornaments of La Granja, the stately royal palace near Segovia.

162 NICOLAS POUSSIN (1594–1665). French. *Parnassus*. Painted 1625–30. Oil on canvas, 57⅛ x 77⅝"

The *Parnassus*, painted in the first years after Poussin's arrival in Rome, owes much to Raphael's painting of the same subject in the Stanza della Segnatura of the Vatican. The reclining nude in the foreground, classical in her proportions and cool remoteness, personifies Castalia, the crystal fountain flowing from the cave of the Delphic oracle. Behind her Calliope crowns Homer who, come to do homage to Apollo, is surrounded by the other muses and poets in carefully arranged groups. The abundance of delicious *amoretti* recalls the crowds of babies in Titian's Bacchanals, now in the Prado (see plates 138 and 139) —pictures which Poussin copied when they were still in Italy.

163 CLAUDE LORRAIN (CLAUDE GELLÉE; 1600–82). French. *Moses Saved from the Nile*. Painted about 1648. Oil on canvas, 82¼ x 54⅜"

French painting seems to have had little appeal for the Royal Spanish collectors, for most of the great French masters of the eighteenth and nineteenth centuries are entirely unrepresented in the Prado. Excellent works, however, by the seventeenth-century artists Poussin (see plates 160–162) and Claude are to be found there. Almost all of the Claudes were brought in by Philip IV, whose taste for quality was so broad that it embraced many different schools of painting.

Claude, whose real surname was Gellée, was born in Lorraine, but like his great compatriot Poussin spent almost all his life in Italy. He concentrated from the beginning of his career on the painting of landscape, responding in Italy to the influence of Agostino Tassi, and to the Northern landscape artists Paul Brill and Adam Elsheimer, who like himself had come from beyond the Alps to work in the South.

At the beginning of his career his color contrasts were strong, but they were soon subdued into poetical harmonies. The beautiful landscapes of his maturity laid stress on stately balance and the tender luminosity which no painter has ever excelled.

He was enormously successful, providing paintings for kings, popes, and cardinals. His pictures were in such great demand that he had to protect himself from dishonest imitators by recording in drawings two hundred of his landscapes made between 1630 and 1678. This collection of drawings, which has belonged since 1770 to the Dukes of Devonshire at Chatsworth, was engraved and published with the title *Liber Veritatis*.

Moses Saved from the Nile is one of a set of four large upright canvases of the same scale painted by Claude for Philip IV, with corresponding drawings in the *Liber Veritatis*. As in all of Claude's most beautiful works, the figures are extremely small in relation to the lofty sweep of sky and distance, conveying an impression that all human activity, no matter how dramatic, is subordinate to the great planned harmony of nature herself.

164 CLAUDE LORRAIN (CLAUDE GELLÉE; 1600–82). French. *The Burial of St. Serapia*. Painted about 1648. Oil on canvas, 83½ x 57⅛"

This painting, like *Moses Saved from the Nile* (plate 163), belonged to the set that Philip IV commissioned Claude to paint for him. St. Serapia, one of the virgin martyrs of the Early Christian church, was a Syrian girl who lived in Italy as the slave of an Umbrian lady named Sabina. Serapia converted her mistress to the new faith, and both Sabina and Serapia have become saints. In the second century of the Christian era, in the year 119 A.D. according to the ancient records, St. Serapia was provoked, near Terni, into administering a rebuff to some libertines, and in return was clubbed cruelly and finally beheaded. Her relics were carried for burial to the church in Rome dedicated to the honor of her mistress, St. Sabina.

Claude has represented the burial taking place in a shadowed spot near the remains of a lofty classical colonnade. The Colosseum may be seen in the hazy middle distance, against a sky so purely lovely as to justify its occupying nearly half of the canvas. Few painters have seen human life so harmoniously poised against a view of nature that comprehends all beauty, dignity, and serenity.

165 JEAN ANTOINE WATTEAU (1684–1721). French. *The Marriage Contract*. Painted 1714. Oil on canvas, 18½ x 21⅝"

Watteau was born in the Franco-Flemish city of Valenciennes. In 1702 at the age of eighteen he arrived in Paris and studied under Claude Gillot, a painter and draftsman of theatrical subjects. Later he worked with

Claude Audran, a decorator who gave him access to the King's collection in the Luxembourg Palace. There he saw and profited much from the series of paintings which Rubens had made almost a century earlier for Marie de Médicis. Still later he was a privileged house guest of Pierre Crozat who owned great Venetian paintings and drawings.

Often he painted scenes from the French theater and the Italian *Commedia dell' Arte,* in which he was apt to introduce his friends dressed in the costumes of the well-known roles. Watteau developed the *fête galante* in which high-born people are shown disporting themselves in romantic gardens and parks with the grace and elegance peculiar to the French civilization of the eighteenth century. Yet for Watteau, the gaiety and romance had a tremulous undertone of melancholy, as though he could never forget that the act must soon end and the curtain be rung down.

Watteau was one of those famous geniuses whose epochal life was crowded into painfully few years. In its brevity, his career recalls those of Mozart, Giorgione, Raphael, and Keats. He epitomized his century with its rococo delicacy and grace, and its new freedom from the pomposity and restraint which had characterized the preceding age. His followers, Lancret, Pater, and Fragonard continued the tone of aristocratic gaiety and artifice which he had set. But these followers evidently held no appeal for the Spanish monarchs, and their paintings are not to be found in the Prado.

This small canvas forms a pair with *The Festivity in a Park* (plate 166); according to one author, they once bore the date 1714. They belonged to Isabella Farnese and were listed in the 1746 inventory of her palace, La Granja.

Seated at a table under the trees is shown a notary, pen in hand and dressed in his black robe of office. With him are seated the bridegroom, the bride's father, and the bride herself, with a wreath of flowers suspended over her head. A gay party with music and dancing is in progress under the trees, as was the old custom on such occasions.

166 JEAN ANTOINE WATTEAU (1684–1721). French. *A Festivity in a Park*. Painted 1714. Oil on canvas, 18⅞ x 22″

In a shadowy park adorned with statues of Ceres and Neptune, amorous couples are strolling. The trees of various sorts cast an inviting shade for the lovers. Watteau is said to have observed the statues in the park of Saint Cloud, but the introduction of the umbrella pine, peculiar to the Mediterranean basin, is a device of romantic exoticism; and practical disposition of the water so copiously pouring from the basin of the fountain of Neptune does not greatly trouble our idyllic painter.

167 JEAN ANTOINE WATTEAU (1684–1721). French. *A Festivity in a Park* (detail of plate 166)

A pair of lovers stands before the Fountain of Neptune; this detail excludes the figure of the sea god, showing only his car drawn by hippocampuses. The lady turns her head toward her lover with an appearance of gentle affection, but he, with hand on hip, an obvious swaggerer, looks beyond her as though demanding approval from the spectator. Characteristic of Watteau is just such a suspenseful situation, tense with half-satisfied emotion.

ACKNOWLEDGEMENTS

The author, and the publisher and his associates express their gratitude to the Prado Museum *and its staff for the many courtesies which have made it possible to produce this book. We are especially indebted to the Museum's distinguished Sub-Director,* Don F. J. Sánchez Cantón *for his interest and for the Foreword which he wrote.*

In a book of art, it seems particularly fitting to acknowledge the work of craftsmen who contribute to its making. The color photography and plates were executed under the direction of Thames & Hudson, *New York and London. Black and white photographs were supplied by* Anderson, Rome, *and* MAS, Barcelona. *The* Flower Electrotype Co., New York, *made the electrotypes from which the illustrations were printed. The color printing is from the presses of* Rogers Kellogg Stillson, Inc., New York. *The type was set by* Westcott & Thomson, Inc., *Philadelphia, and the text was printed by* The Murray Printing Company, Wakefield, Massachusetts. *The* H. Wolff Book Manufacturing Co., New York, *bound the book and* Perkins and Squier, New York *supplied the paper.*